ENTERPRISE SECURITY SERIES

ZSCALER:

Through the Execution Lens™

How Enterprise Programs Deliver Zero Trust at Scale

A PRACTITIONER'S GUIDE

A Companion to Cloud Migration PM Bible™

Zero Trust | The Execution Lens™ Framework

GÉRALD L'OUVERTURE NOËL

BA in Psychology — Hofstra University
Project Management Certificate — Cornell University

Leadership Coach — John Maxwell Team

PMP® — Project Management Institute (PMI)

ZSCALER: Through the Execution Lens™ represents the culmination of his experience, research, and structured approach to enterprise transformation.

Copyright

ISBN: 979-8-234-09444-5

www.cloudmigrationpmplaybook.com

Dedication

To the builders of control—

the IT leaders
and project management professionals
who operate where systems are not theoretical,
but real.

Who carry responsibility
when architecture meets pressure.

Who understand—

that execution is not support.

It is the outcome.

Acknowledgement

To my wife, **Nilufar Yasmin Noel**—
for standing beside the work
long before it had a name,

and long after it became one.

You understood what I could not yet articulate—
that I was meant to be built,

fully and without compromise.

You did not question the path.

You protected it.

And in doing so—

you made the work possible.

Acknowledgement

To **Alan Dumitras**, a friend I met late in life—
yet one who feels as though he has walked beside me for years.

We share the same birthday—
but more than that, we share a quiet understanding
that time does not always define connection.

You saw something I did not yet name—
the intensity, the conviction, the quiet fire
when I spoke about Zscaler.

And in a simple moment, you said—
write the book.

In that moment, the idea became reality.
In your words, innovation is rooted in us—this book is its execution lens.

A Note to the Reader

He who influences the thought of his times influences the times that follow.
— *Elbert Hubbard*

This is a choice of free will—
a choice belonging only to mankind—
to allow,
and to disallow.

I allow few philosophers to influence my thought—
for certain teachings must survive ignorance—
which, at times, proves a greater force than nature itself.

This book is written in a nontraditional way—and for a purpose.
Words must be digested—not merely consumed—if they are to carry weight.
That is why I write in short sentences—and employ the em dash with deliberate intent.

The em dash is not decoration.
It is emphasis.
It is weight.
It is pause.

Each em dash signals a moment to process—to reflect—to connect one thought to the next.

The subjects explored in this book are complex—and complex ideas deserve room to breathe.

Environments and systems must be governed with discipline and precision.
Accuracy demands calculation.

Speed demands restraint.

Both require judgment.

In matters of execution—whether of technology, leadership, or human decision—the smallest oversight often carries the greatest consequence.

Nothing is new under the sun.

TABLE OF CONTENTS

Preface

Before the Lens

This book is not a continuation of Cloud Migration PM Bible™.

It is a consequence of it.

Every program that failed—
not at the technology level,
but at the execution level—
left a pattern.

Not a lesson.

A pattern.

Patterns do not require reflection
to be useful.

They require recognition.

This book is about recognition.

Zscaler is not the subject.

Execution is.

Zscaler is the environment
in which execution either holds—
or collapses.

Zero Trust is not a product decision.

It is a program discipline.

And discipline, unlike technology,
cannot be purchased.

It must be built—

deliberately,

sequentially,

and under pressure.

The Execution Lens™ is the framework
that makes that building possible.

> ***Strategy defines direction. Execution determines survivability.***

This visual representation is more than a diagram—It is a lens.

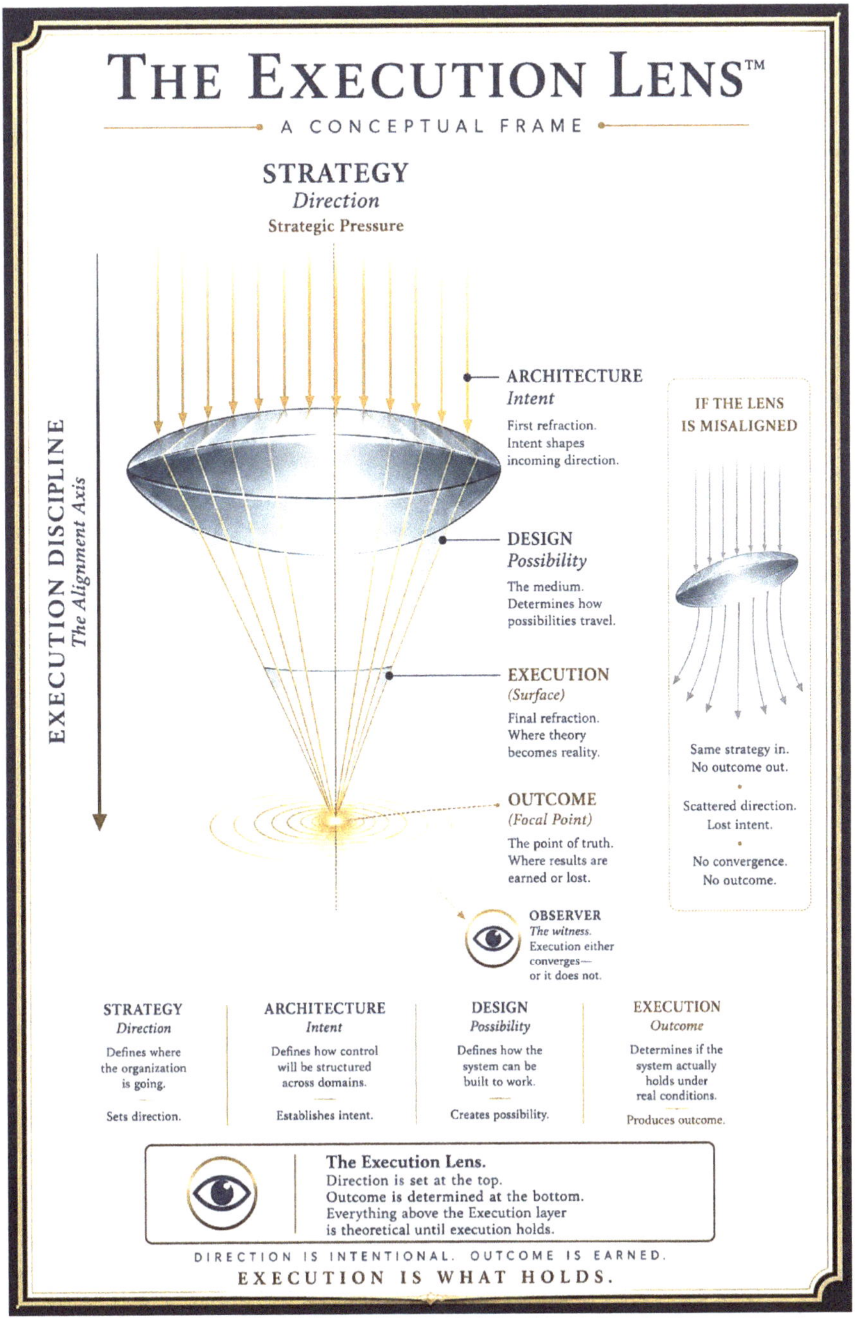

Everything that follows—is viewed through that lens.

What follows is not theory.

It is the record of what happens.

when Zero Trust architecture meets enterprise reality—
and what it takes to survive that meeting.

And what that reality reveals—
is often misunderstood
before it is ever executed.

That is where most organizations begin
to question the platform—
instead of the discipline
required to implement it.

This book does not answer that.

It reframes it.

So that when execution begins—
the outcome is no longer left to assumption.

It is governed—
By discovery,
By discipline,
And by control.

Gérald L'Ouverture Noël

"Vouloir, c'est pouvoir."

To will—
is to be able.

Introduction

Zscaler is often described in one word:

Complex.

And that description is not wrong.

But it is incomplete.

Because complexity is not the problem.

Misunderstanding is.

Organizations do not struggle with Zscaler because it is too advanced.

They struggle because it demands something most environments are not built to provide.

Discipline.

Zero Trust is not a feature set.

It is not a deployment.

And it is not a product decision.

It is a shift in how control is defined,

enforced,

and sustained—
under real conditions.

That shift is where most implementations fail.

Not in architecture.
Not in design.
In execution.

There is a question that quietly follows Zscaler
in almost every organization:

Has it ever been fully implemented?

And when that question is asked—
it is often interpreted as doubt.

A warning.

A reason to hesitate.

It should not be.

Because the absence of "complete implementation"
is not a failure of the platform.

It is a reflection of the environment
attempting to implement it.

Zscaler does not fail because it is complex.

It fails because it exposes.

What was never structured to begin with:

Undocumented dependencies
Incomplete application discovery
Fragmented ownership
Inconsistent enforcement
Assumptions mistaken for control

In that sense—

Zscaler does not introduce difficulty.

It reveals it.

And that revelation is often mistaken
for the problem itself.

It is not the cause.

It is the beginning of control.

Organizations looking to implement Zscaler
often ask the wrong question:

"How do we deploy it?"

The correct question is:

"Are we prepared to operate it?"

Because Zscaler does not sit on top of chaos
and organize it.

It forces the organization
to organize itself.

Before policy can be enforced—
ownership must be defined.

Before access can be controlled—
application discovery must be complete.

Before Zero Trust can be declared—
control must exist.

That is why this book exists.

Not to explain Zscaler as a product.

But to establish Zscaler
as an execution discipline.

This is not a guide to configuration.

It is a guide to control.

Because in the end—
Zscaler does not fail
because it is too complex.

It fails because execution was never structured
to sustain it.

And when execution changes—
the outcome changes.

The Lens Changes the View

Every architecture—
changes what the organization sees.

But some architectures
do something more dangerous.

They change
what the organization can no longer ignore.

Zscaler is one of them.

Because Zero Trust
does not merely alter access.

It alters perception.

What once appeared controlled—
may no longer appear secure.

What once appeared functional—
may reveal hidden instability.

What once appeared trusted—
may only have been reachable.

That is where the lens begins.

PART I

The Emergence of the Execution Lens

How the discipline of execution became the determining factor in modern security transformation.

Chapter 1

Before I Knew the Name, I Knew the Discipline

I did not learn Zscaler in a classroom—
not through instruction,
not through structured teaching.

I did not discover it in a certification program—
not through validation,
not through formal recognition.

And I did not arrive at it through theory—
not through models,
not through conceptual understanding.

I was already practicing it—
already executing,
already operating within it.

Before I knew it—
Before I could name it.
Before I could define it.

Before I understood its complexity—
I already felt its weight,
already lived what it truly was.

> ***Structure determines outcome.***

Not effort.
Not intention.
Not even intelligence.
Structure—above all.

If something needed to be done, I would break it down—
not react,
not improvise blindly—
reduce it,
structure it,
make it controllable.

If it broke, I would trace it back—
not guess,
not patch—
follow the path,
identify the origin,
understand the chain.

If it failed, I would find where control was lost—
not accept failure as outcome—
locate the breakdown,
expose the gap,
restore control.

At the time, I did not call it governance—
no formal language,
no institutional framing.

I did not call it execution—
no defined discipline,
no structured methodology.

And I certainly did not call it project management—
no label,
no title,
no system attached to it.

But that is exactly what it was—
not something new,
not something learned later—
something already real,
already in motion,
already true.

Years later, that instinct evolved into something formal—
what was intuitive
became structured,
what was practiced
became documented.

Documented, structured, and eventually published in *Cloud Migration PM Bible*™—
not invented—
codified.

That work was never about cloud alone—
not infrastructure,
not technology—

but something deeper:

How complex systems move—
from one state to another—
without collapsing under its own weight.

Infrastructure and migration became my first true discipline—
not by coincidence, but by alignment.
Because every system, no matter how sophisticated,
depends on its foundation.

You can redesign applications.
You can modernize interfaces.
You can even transform business models.

But if the foundation is unstable—
everything above it inherits that instability.
That is why I was drawn to infrastructure.

That is why I was drawn to migration.

And ultimately—
that is why I was drawn to Zscaler.

But my introduction to Zscaler was not strategic.
It was not planned.
And it certainly was not elegant.

It was naive—
dangerously so.

I knew of Zscaler.
I had heard the name.
I understood, at a high level, what it was supposed to represent.

But I did not know Zscaler.

Not until the moment it nearly cost me my credentials.

1. 1 The Engagement That Forced the Education

It happened during a state government engagement—
a large-scale organizational separation. A statutory split.

Two entities, once operating as one,
now forced to divide:
Infrastructure,
Identity access,
Operational control—
under pressure,
under time constraints,
and under political scrutiny.

> ***These are the moments where architecture stops being theory—
> and becomes consequence.***

This was not a lab.
This was not a greenfield implementation.

This was a live enterprise fracture.

Systems had to remain active.
Critical applications could not become inoperative.
Endpoints had to be brought to a supported Windows 11 enterprise baseline—aligned with security and policy enforcement requirements.

And the transfer itself had to occur—
without introducing operational instability.

That kind of migration teaches a brutal truth:

> ***A successful pilot does not prove a successful rollout.***

Pilots are controlled.
They are executed with the most prepared population in the environment—engineers, IT teams, people who understand the tooling.

Production is different.

Production introduces inconsistency.
Production introduces unmanaged variation.
Production introduces endpoints that are not as current as assumed—and applications that are far less tolerant than documented.

1.2 The ZCC Failure and What It Revealed

As part of the transfer, the security posture had to be handled live.
Zscaler could not be decommissioned early—
and rightly so.

Because during a migration, the environment is often at its weakest point:

systems are changing
controls are shifting
trust boundaries are being redrawn

In that window—

exposure can emerge.

That is precisely why security controls must remain intact
until the exact moment of transition.

In our case, the Zscaler stack had to be decommissioned
on the day of transfer—

as part of the live cutover sequence.

Not before.

ZIA and ZPA were manageable.

Those components transitioned as expected.

ZCC did not.

Zscaler Client Connector did not cleanly disengage.

It behaved like a ghost in the environment—
reappearing, persisting,
failing to fully release control at the endpoint layer.

And that changed everything.

In a live migration, time is not abstract.

Every minute of instability consumes coordination capital.

Engineers are on bridge calls.
Vendors are engaged.
Stakeholders are waiting.
Dependent workstreams are blocked.

And the longer one control remains unresolved—
the more the entire migration begins to destabilize.

1.3 Rollback Is a Leadership Discipline

We reached the point where persistence was no longer responsible.
We rolled back.

And this is where leadership maturity reveals itself—
in the ability to tolerate pause,
to resist the pressure of forced progress,
and to choose control over momentum.

> ***Rollback is not failure. Rollback is controlled reversion.***

Not retreat—
but a deliberate pause in forward motion.

Time to restore.
Time to recalibrate.
Time to understand what the system is actually telling us.

And only then—
does execution resume with clarity.

Rollback is control.

We stabilized the environment.
We preserved operations.
And we bought ourselves the time to understand what actually happened.

It took approximately two days of coordinated analysis
to isolate the issue.

The problem was not a simple failure of tooling.

It was an intersection:

Endpoint enforcement behavior
Windows 11 baseline alignment
Policy persistence at the client level
Enterprise control dependencies

These layers had not been fully neutralized
prior to the live event.

Through alignment with Zscaler operational guidance and SOP,
we identified the resolution path—
and reattempted the transition under controlled conditions.

We lived to make it to another day.

From that point forward, the migration did not proceed by assumption.

It proceeded by control—

by departments;
by sites;
by deliberate sequencing.

We still encountered issues.

Of course we did.

Real enterprise migrations always do.

But the lesson had already been burned in:

> ***A pilot proves possibility. It does not prove enterprise readiness.***

And a control you do not fully understand—
especially at the endpoint—
can humble an entire migration
faster than any status report can explain.

1.4 The Line Between Product and Reality

That was the moment Zscaler stopped being a product name to me.
It became an execution reality.

Not marketing.
Not architecture in abstraction.
Not theory from a diagram.

Reality.

Because in that moment, I saw something clearly—
not as a product comparison,
not as a vendor decision—
but as a structural truth:

> ***Access, when poorly designed, becomes the fastest path to exposure.***

This book is not about Zscaler as a product.
It is about Zscaler as a moment of realization.

A shift.

A line between how organizations believe they control access—
and how access actually behaves under pressure.

And that is where the Execution Lens™ begins.

Because what that moment revealed—
was not just a failure of tooling.

It revealed something deeper:
Control does not fail at the surface.
It fails at the foundation.

And if that foundation is not understood—
no architecture above it can be trusted to hold.

That is where the next chapter begins.

Chapter 2

Infrastructure as the First Language of Control

Control does not begin at the application layer.

It does not begin with user experience.
And it does not begin with security tooling.

Control begins at the foundation.

> ***Control does not fail at the surface. It fails at the foundation—and only reveals itself at the surface.***

In enterprise environments, that foundation is infrastructure.

Infrastructure is not visible to most users.
It does not define how systems look.
It does not shape how interfaces behave.

But it determines whether anything functions at all.

Every system—
no matter how advanced—
depends on infrastructure.

Compute must exist.
Not as an idea.

Not as something provisioned on paper.

But as real, running capacity—
servers, virtual machines, or cloud services
that are powered on, reachable,
and capable of executing work.

If nothing is there to process instructions—nothing runs.

If there is nothing capable of executing instructions,
the system does not exist—no matter what the design says.

Networks must route correctly.

Systems must be able to find each other.

If data cannot travel from one point to another,
the system is not connected—
it is isolated.

Identity must resolve.

Users and systems must be recognized and authenticated.

If identity fails, access fails—
even if everything else is functioning.

Dependencies must be reachable.

Applications rely on other systems—databases, APIs, services.

If those connections break,
the application may still exist—

but it cannot function.

When infrastructure is stable, systems appear reliable.
When infrastructure is unstable,
everything above it inherits that instability.

That is why control cannot be defined at the surface.
It must be established—at the base.

2.1 Architecture Designs. Infrastructure Decides.

Architecture describes intention.
Infrastructure determines outcome.

This distinction is not theoretical.
It is operational.

Systems rarely fail because the design was wrong.

They fail because the conditions required to support that design
were never fully understood.

And those conditions—
are governed by infrastructure.

Architecture can describe a secure system.
Infrastructure determines whether that system can survive
under real conditions.

Design intent does not fail.
Execution conditions do.

And execution conditions are governed by infrastructure—
not by what was planned,
but by what was built,
configured,
and maintained.

That is where migration becomes the first real discipline of control—
because it alone forces the truth about infrastructure to surface.

2.2 Migration Does Not expose Systems. It Exposes The Truth About Them. Designs.

Migration is not simply movement.
It is the controlled transition of systems
from one state to another—
without breaking dependencies,
without losing access,
and without destabilizing operations.

Every migration exposes reality:
Undocumented dependencies.
Inconsistent configurations.
Hidden assumptions.

And it does so under conditions
where failure has immediate impact.

That is why migration is not just a technical exercise.
It is an execution discipline.

It forces clarity.

It removes abstraction.

And it reveals where control actually exists—

not where it is assumed to exist.

When systems move:

Control must persist
Access must remain consistent
Enforcement must behave predictably

If any of those conditions fail—

the system does not degrade gracefully.

It breaks.

2.3 Design vs. Execution — The Defining Difference

You do not understand a system because it works.

You understand it when it is forced to change.

Design defines how a system should behave.

Infrastructure determines whether it can.

Migration reveals the difference.

This is the first moment where control is tested.

Not in theory.
Not in diagrams.

But in execution.

Understanding this is not optional.

It is what separates controlled execution
from operational instability.

2.4 The Foundation Zscaler Operates On

Zscaler does not replace this foundation.

It operates on top of it.

If the foundation is misunderstood—

the implementation will reflect that misunderstanding.

Everything that follows—

how access is enforced,
how policies are applied,
how Zero Trust is installed

depends on it.

Infrastructure is not just a layer.

It is the first language of control.

Chapter 3

The Moment Zscaler Became Real

Zscaler does not become real during design. It does not become real during planning. And it does not become real during a successful pilot.

> ***Zscaler becomes real at the exact moment control is tested.***

That moment is not theoretical.
It is operational.

It is where dependencies surface.
Where assumptions collapse.
Where control must prove itself—under live conditions.

At that point, the question is no longer:
"What is Zscaler designed to do?"

The question becomes:
Where does control actually exist?
How is access truly enforced?
What happens when that control behaves differently than expected?

That is the line between architecture and execution.

And most organizations cross that line unprepared.

3.1 The Ownership Problem No One Solves

Before implementation fails—
ownership already has.
Zscaler is indeed a cybersecurity control platform.

It defines:
Access policy.
Enforcement logic.
Risk boundaries.
Compliance posture.

> ***That responsibility belongs—clearly—to Security.***

Not to infrastructure.
Not to network.
Not to the CIO by default.

Security must own Zscaler.

Because control—
at its core—is a security function.

But execution does not follow ownership.

Zscaler spans across multiple operational domains:
Network behavior.
Identity validation.
Endpoint enforcement.
Traffic routing.

Each domain is owned by a different team.

Each team operates with:

Different priorities.

Different tools.

Different assumptions.

This creates a structural gap—

not in technology—

but in responsibility.

Zscaler may originate within Security.

But its execution extends across the enterprise.

When that distinction is not enforced—

failure is not random.

It follows patterns.

Zscaler is not a typical implementation.

It is an aberration—

in how enterprise systems are designed,
owned,
and executed.

An aberrational project does not follow
historical patterns.

It breaks them.

Zscaler does exactly that.

It inverts the trust model—
from network to identity.

It expands the dependency chain—
across identity,
endpoint,
DNS,
routing,
and policy.

It removes the idea of a single controlling domain.

And replaces it—
with shared execution across the enterprise.
That is why ownership becomes unstable.

Not because ownership is unclear—
but because the system itself
does not conform to traditional boundaries.

And when an aberrational system
is managed as if it were ordinary—
the failure is already set in motion.

Failure Pattern 1 — Misplaced Ownership

Zscaler is owned outside Security.

Policy loses depth.
Risk is misunderstood.
Enforcement becomes technical—
not risk-driven.
Control exists—
but it is disconnected
from security intent.

Failure Pattern 2 — Distributed Ownership

Zscaler is shared—without authority.

Policies are defined in isolation.
Enforcement behaves inconsistently.
Accountability dissolves.

Contribution increases.

Ownership disappears.

Failure Pattern 3 — Ownership Without Execution Alignment

Security owns Zscaler—

but does not align
with infrastructure,

identity,

or endpoint teams.

Dependencies are misunderstood.

Execution breaks across domains.

Delivery slows—

under coordination friction.

Ownership exists—

but execution is disconnected.

▶ **Real-World Execution Signal**

An access failure is reported.

The network team confirms routing is correct.

The identity team confirms authentication is successful.

The endpoint team confirms the client is functioning.

Security confirms policy is configured.

And yet—

the user cannot access the application.

Because the failure does not exist in one domain. It exists in the interaction between them.

Without clear ownership:
Resolution slows
Accountability diffuses
Risk compounds

> ***Control without ownership is not control. It is isolation.***

Effective control requires both—

clear ownership

and coordinated execution.

Ownership defines accountability.

But it does not eliminate uncertainty.

Because even with perfect ownership—
one question remains:

What exactly are we trying to control?

And that question—
is not answered in execution.

It is answered in discovery and strategy—
before execution begins.

3.2 Zscaler Changes What Control Means

Traditional enterprise control
is anchored in the network.

If the network is controlled—
access is assumed to be controlled.

VPN extended that model.

It did not redefine it.

Users connected to the network—
and once connected—
trust was implicitly granted.

That model depends on a single premise:
location determines trust.

Zscaler removes that premise—
entirely.

Control is no longer anchored to the network.

It is defined through:
Identity
Policy
Endpoint enforcement

The network still exists.

Traffic still flows.

But it is no longer trusted
as the place where access is decided.

What That Actually Means

This must be stated precisely:

Traditional IPsec and full-tunnel
remote-access VPNs
generally, extend Layer 3 network reachability
into the private environment.

That reachability is subsequently constrained—
by routing,
transport-layer ports,
firewall policy,
segmentation,
and application controls.

ZPA operates differently.

It enforces application-centric access—
rather than granting general
network-level reachability.

Policies identify private applications

through defined attributes—
including hostname,
IP address,
port,
protocol,
identity,
device posture,
and contextual conditions.

VPN extends connectivity.
ZPA brokers controlled access.

A traditional VPN may place the endpoint
within a routable private-network context.
ZPA does not provide
that same general network membership.

It does not create
a traditional network-extension tunnel
that places the user
directly onto the private network.

In practice—
it brokers access
to specifically authorized
application destinations.

The scope of that access
is determined by the application definition,
policy design,
identity context,
device posture,
and the dependencies included
within the application segment.

The Truth That Must Be Understood

Zscaler does not secure the network at the IP layer—
because it is not designed to operate at that layer.

This is not weakness.

It is design.

Zscaler removes network-layer trust—
and replaces it with application-level control.

But in doing so—
it leaves certain behaviors
outside its boundary.

And what sits outside that boundary—
does not disappear.

It becomes the responsibility of the program
to identify, classify,
and decide how it will be handled.

Because anything not understood at this stage—
will not be discovered in design.

It will be discovered—
in execution.

Zero Trust Evaluation Model

In Zero Trust, access is evaluated continuously—
based on who the user is.

What they are allowed to access.

Whether current conditions permit it.
Authorization express intent.
Enforcement decides reality.

Control Behavior in Execution

This shift changes behavior—

Not just architecture.

In the traditional model—
the VPN-driven model:
Control is static.
Trust is granted once,
and enforcement is assumed.

In the Zscaler model:
Control is continuous,
Trust is evaluated per request,
and enforcement is dynamic.

That shift has consequences in execution:

Access can succeed in one moment—
and fail in the next.

Policy decisions are not permanent.

User experience reflects real-time conditions.

Organizations expect control

to behave like infrastructure—

Stable.

Predictable.

Fixed.

Zero Trust does not behave that way.

It behaves like execution.

Conditional.
Context-aware.
Continuously enforced.

▶ Real-World Execution Signal — "It Worked Yesterday"

A user reports:

"It worked yesterday—but not today."

In a traditional model—

this suggests instability.

In a Zero Trust model—

this reflects evaluation.

Something changed—

device posture,

identity context,

policy condition,

access path—

and the system responded accordingly.

That is not failure.

That is control behaving as designed.

The Control Boundary Reality — VPN vs. ZPA

There is a critical distinction that must be understood before attempting to fully replace VPN with Zscaler.

VPN says:
"You are on the network."

ZPA says:
"You are allowed to this application."

Those are not the same outcome.

Under VPN:
The user gains network reachability:
The endpoint receives an IP address.
It can ping.
It can scan.
It can route—
and reach systems at the network layer.

The network is exposed.

Under ZPA:
The user gains permission
to specifically authorized
application destinations.

Access is granted only
to explicitly defined applications
and their permitted dependencies.

The endpoint is not given
general membership
in the private network.

The user does not receive
broad network reachability
beyond what policy and
application definitions permit.

This materially reduces
user-originated network discovery
and lateral-movement opportunities—

because the endpoint is not permitted
to traverse the broader internal network.

But it does not eliminate
every possible form of lateral movement.

Exposure may still arise—
through compromised application servers,
overly broad application segments,
service accounts,
shared administrative credentials,
application dependencies,
workload compromise,
or another authorized access path.

And the model itself
introduces a boundary.

The Residual Capability Gap

Because ZPA does not grant
general Layer 3 network reachability
to the user endpoint—

certain network-level capabilities
do not exist in the same way:

ICMP diagnostics — ping, traceroute.

Raw IP communication.

Network scanning and discovery.

Server-initiated protocols.

Subnet routing behavior.

Site-to-site connectivity.

> ***These are not security failures. They are architectural differences. And in some environments, they matter.***

It does not imply Zscaler is incomplete—

only that it operates differently.

These capabilities do not disappear.

They remain—
embedded in systems,
embedded in workflows,
embedded in assumptions.

And when they are not accounted for—

they do not fail during design.

They fail—

when execution begins.

The Practitioner Responsibility

For the Technical Project Manager, this must be addressed early.

Discovery must identify:
Network-layer dependencies.
Protocol constraints.
Legacy behaviors.
Hidden assumptions.

Strategy must define:
What Zscaler replaces.
What it does not replace.
Where coexistence remains necessary.
How uncovered use cases will be handled.

Execution must ensure:
No critical functionality is lost.
No assumptions survive untested.
No hidden dependencies surface during rollout.

Because rollout does not reveal everything.

It reveals only what was not discovered.

And what is not discovered—

does not wait.

It surfaces—under pressure.

Closing Principle

Zscaler does not change where control exists.

It changes how control behaves—
and where it is enforced.

Organizations that fail to understand that shift
do not fail because of the technology.

They fail because they continue to operate
under a model of control
that no longer applies.

That is the moment Zscaler becomes real.

Not as a concept.

Not as a platform.

But as execution—
that exposes what was never fully understood.

And once exposed—
those gaps do not resolve themselves.

They must be discovered.

They must be defined.

And they must be controlled—
before execution attempts to enforce them.

Because what is not defined—

will not be governed.

And what is not governed—
will fail when system is placed under real conditions.

And when it fails—
it reveals something deeper:
that access was never understood
to begin with.

PART II

The Strategic Lens

Access is not the same as control. This section examines the architectural decisions that determine where control actually lives—and where, without discipline, it disappears.

Chapter 4

The Illusion of Access

Access is one of the most misunderstood concepts in enterprise security.

That failure—

is rarely technical.

It is conceptual.

It exposes something

most organizations never define correctly—

access.

Organizations invest significantly in enabling access—

remote connectivity,

cloud adoption,

identity platforms,

endpoint management.

The assumption behind that investment is simple:

if a user can reach a system,

control has been achieved.

That assumption—

is the illusion.

Reachability and control are not equivalent constructs.

A user who can connect to a system
is not necessarily a user whose access has been evaluated,

enforced,
or contained.

The ability to reach a resource
does not prove:
that the reach was authorized,
that the access was appropriate,
or that the session was governed.

This distinction is not theoretical.
It becomes visible—
when the architecture is tested under pressure.

> ***The question is never whether access works. The question is whether access is controlled.***

The transition from VPN-based architecture to Zero Trust
is not a simple technology replacement.

It is a reorientation—
of where control is placed,
how trust is evaluated,
and what access actually means.

Organizations that treat this transition as a product swap—
replacing one tool with another—
inherit the same structural vulnerabilities
they meant to remove.

They end up with new technology—
operating under old assumptions.

New tools
do not eliminate old thinking—
architecture does.

4.1 Network Reachability vs. Application Access

The distinction between network
reachability
and application access
is the architectural foundation
on which Zero Trust is built.

Understanding it is not optional—
it is the prerequisite
for every implementation decision
that follows.

Traditional enterprise access models were built around a single premise:
Secure the network—
and access is controlled.

That logic produced the perimeter model—
a trusted inside,
an untrusted outside,
and a boundary that defined both.

VPN extended that model into remote work.

When users needed access from outside
the office,
VPN recreated the internal experience—

traffic was tunneled
into the corporate environment.

Once inside—
the user received a private IP address
and gained Layer 3 reachability.

The ability to communicate—
with anything routing allowed.

This model carries a structural characteristic
that matters:
Access comes before definition.
The user joins the network first.
Application access is determined later—
by what is reachable.

Authentication becomes the threshold.

Network placement becomes the proxy for authorization.

> ***VPN grants presence on the network. Zero Trust grants access to an application. These are architecturally distinct outcomes.***

Zscaler Private Access (ZPA)
operates on a different principle entirely.

It does not grant the user
general membership in the private network.

It does not provide the endpoint
with broad routable access

to the internal environment.
And it does not create
a traditional network-extension tunnel
through which the user can freely traverse
the private network.

Instead—
it brokers authorized application sessions
through encrypted connections—
through the ZPA cloud,
and through outbound App Connector paths.

The private network is not presented
to the user as a generally reachable access surface.

The user does not receive
unrestricted network-level reachability.

Access remains limited
to the application destinations,
ports,
protocols,
identities,
and conditions
authorized by policy.

That distinction—
has consequences.

Immediate ones.

Operational ones.

Unavoidable ones.

Diagnostics change.

What could once be tested
with a simple ping
or traceroute—
no longer validates
the same way.

Engineers must shift
from network-level troubleshooting
to application-level validation.

Assumptions break.

Applications that "always worked" over VPN—
because the network was reachable—
fail under ZPA.

Dependencies were never explicitly defined.

Hidden connections surface.

Backend APIs.
Authentication services.
Database calls.

All the paths
that were silently allowed—
must now be declared.

Or they fail.

Access becomes precise.

Users no longer "have access to the network."

They have access—
only to what is defined.

Nothing more.

And nothing adjacent.

Lateral movement disappears.

But so does flexibility.

What was once loosely connected—
must now be intentionally designed.

Execution slows—
not because the model is inefficient,
but because the truth is now visible.

And what was hidden—
must be resolved.

ZPA does not introduce complexity. It reveals it.

What VPN Provides at the Network Layer

When a user connects through VPN—the endpoint joins the corporate network.

It becomes part of the topology.
It receives an IP address.
And with that address comes network capability—

the same kind
a machine physically sitting inside the office
would have.

IP routing.
Subnet reachability.

Corporate routers now forward traffic
to internal networks they already trust.

Finance.
Engineering.
HR.

Not merely
the application the user came for.

ICMP diagnostics—

ping.
traceroute.

The endpoint can discover which hosts are alive.
Map the paths between them.

Useful for troubleshooting.

Equally useful
for reconnaissance.

Port-level service access.

Every running service listens on a port.

SSH.
Databases.
File shares.
Remote desktop.

VPN exposes these services
at the network layer—

before the application itself
gets to ask who is connecting.

Network scanning.

From inside the topology—

the endpoint can sweep address ranges,
enumerate services,
and discover exposed systems.

The network responds—

because it assumes
the requester belongs.

Legacy protocol compatibility.

Older protocols were designed
for trusted LAN environments.

SMB.
RDP.
LDAP.
NetBIOS.

Some authenticate weakly.

Some were never designed
for hostile environments at all.

VPN places the endpoint
directly inside the trust boundary
those protocols expect.

Site-to-site communication.

VPN does not always connect
a single user.

Sometimes—

it connects entire networks.

A foothold in one location
can now reach systems
in another.

This breadth was intentional.

The assumption was simple:

if you are inside—
you are trusted.

The consequence—

is lateral movement.

A user — or attacker—
can move beyond the intended destination.

Traverse the network.

Explore what should not be exposed.

Not necessarily
by breaking anything—

but by using the access
the network layer already granted.

What ZPA Provides at the Application Layer

ZPA provides
an application-centric access model.

It does not extend
general private-network membership
to the user endpoint.

Instead—
it creates a brokered access path
between an authorized user or device
and a defined private application.

The application may use
web or non-web protocols—
including TCP- and UDP-based services.

But the access decision

is expressed through the application—
not through unrestricted network placement.

Access is determined
through application segments
and policy conditions that define:

What the application is.
Who may access it.
From which device.
Through which ports and protocols.
And under what conditions.

If an application is not defined
and authorized through policy—

it is not presented to the user
as an accessible destination
through that ZPA access path.

This materially reduces
user-originated network discovery
and lateral movement—
by design.

The endpoint is not given
a broadly traversable private network.

There is no general subnet surface
for the user to scan.

There is no unrestricted network adjacency
for the endpoint to exploit.

But application-level compromise,
workload-to-workload movement,
excessive segment scope,

and alternative access paths
must still be controlled separately.

When the network
is no longer presented to the user
as a broadly reachable access surface—

traditional assumptions
about network placement and implicit trust
disappear with it.

Capabilities disappear:

ICMP diagnostics.
raw IP access.
network scanning.
legacy protocol behavior.

These are not limitations.

They are consequences—

of removing implicit trust.

Architectural Comparison: VPN vs. ZPA

VPN (AnyConnect Model)	ZPA (Zero Trust Model)
Generally, extends Layer 3 network reachability through an encrypted remote-access tunnel	Provides application-centric, policy-brokered access without granting general network membership
Access is further constrained through routing, ports, firewalls, segmentation, and application controls	Applications are defined through hostname or IP, ports, protocols, identity, device posture, and policy context
User joins the corporate network	User is not given general membership in the corporate network
Network IP address assigned to endpoint	No IP address assignment to endpoint
Broad network reachability within VPN scope	Access limited to explicitly defined applications
Trust granted at authentication; implicit thereafter	Trust evaluated continuously per session
Lateral movement possible within network range	User-originated lateral movement materially reduced by design
Network layer is exposed and traversable	The network is not presented to the user as a reachable access surface
ICMP, ping, traceroute function normally	ICMP-based diagnostics not supported
Legacy IP-bound protocols generally supported	Legacy protocols may require alternative access paths
Discovery happens after access is granted	Discovery is required before access is granted

This comparison is not about superiority.

It is about difference.

And misunderstanding that difference—
is where implementation fails.

The Executive Misunderstanding of Access Models

At the executive level—
Zero Trust is often framed as a replacement.

Old technology out.

New technology in.

That framing is incomplete.
And dangerous.

Because what is removed—
is not always understood.

Executives may approve ZPA—
believing VPN is replaced.

Without realizing—
certain behaviors
diagnostics
and dependencies
no longer exist.

When those gaps surface—

they do not appear as minor issues.

They appear as disruption.

> ***The practitioner's responsibility is to define: what is being replaced, what is not, what must coexist, what requires redesign—before execution begins.***

That definition—
is not optional.

It is discovery.

And without it—
execution will fail under pressure.

4.2 ZIA vs. ZPA — Separation of Control Planes

Zscaler operates on two control planes.

Not one.

Each layer answers a different question—
questions that define control itself.

Not how access works—
but how it is governed.

What leaves the organization—
and whether it should.

Who reaches what—
and whether they are entitled.

Whether the device itself can be trusted
to make that request.

Those questions—
are not answered once.

They are answered continuously.

And they determine
whether access is controlled—
or assumed.

They are not interchangeable.

They are complementary.

In execution, this separation stops being theory. The diagram below shows what it becomes.

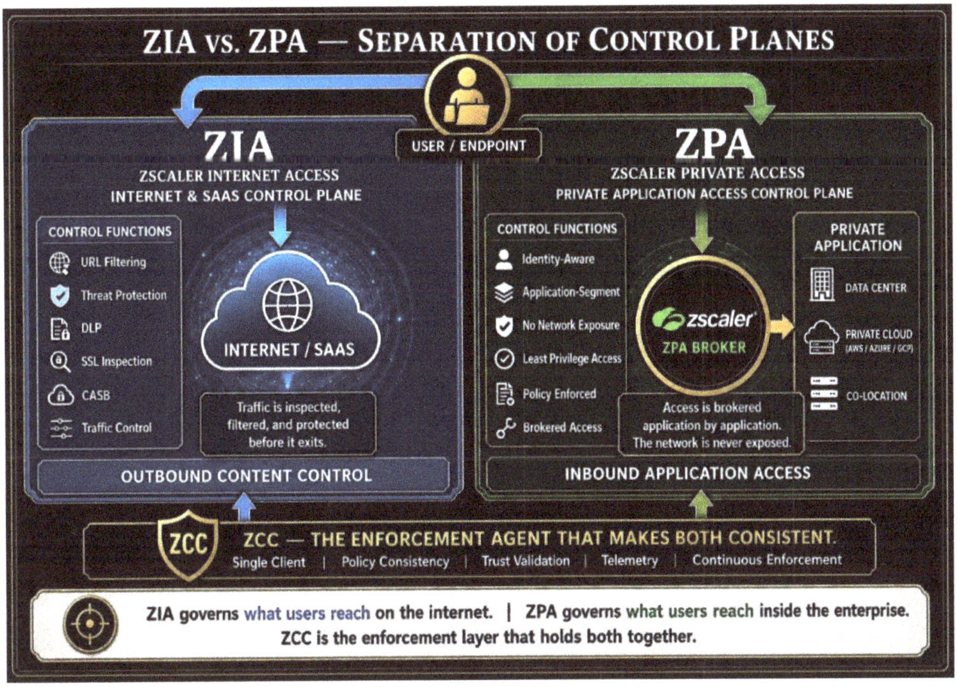

This is where control becomes visible. Not in movement—but in enforcement.

> ***A control plane is not where traffic moves—***
> ***It is where authority is defined.***

ZIA — The Internet and SaaS Control Plane

Zscaler Internet Access (ZIA) is a cloud-native security service that governs all outbound internet and SaaS traffic from the enterprise.

ZIA governs what leaves:

Internet traffic.
SaaS access.

It inspects—

Filters,

and protects.

SSL inspection
URL filtering
malware detection
DLP
CASB
traffic control

ZIA does not govern private applications.

Its scope—

is the outside.

ZPA — The Private Application Access Control Plane

Zscaler Private Access (ZPA)

governs access

to applications hosted in private

environments—

corporate data centers,

private cloud infrastructure

(AWS, Azure, GCP private workloads),

and co-location facilities.

ZPA replaces the function of VPN for user-

to-application access.

It governs what is reached.

Private applications.
Internal services.

The network is never expose.

Access is brokered—

application by application.

Defined through:

Application Segments
Segment Groups
Policies
App Connectors

If it is not defined—

it is not reachable.

This is the inversion of VPN.

VPN exposes everything—

then restricts.

ZPA exposes nothing—

until defined.

Why Zero Trust Requires Separation of Control Planes

The separation between ZIA and ZPA

is not a product architecture choice—

it reflects

the structural requirement

of Zero Trust.

Different traffic—

requires different control.

Internet traffic needs:

Inspection.
Content awareness,
and data protection.

Private access needs:

Identity validation.
Authorization.
And least privilege.

> ***One control plane cannot govern both traffic domains with consistent enforcement. Separation is not a strategy—it is a necessity.***

The Deployment Implication

For the practitioner
the separation of ZIA and ZPA
has a direct deployment consequence.

Each control plane must be:

Discovered.
Configured.
And validated—
independently.

ZIA requires:

Policy definition.
SSL strategy.
Traffic forwarding (GRE, IPSec, PAC, ZCC).
And SaaS governance.

ZPA requires:

Application discovery.
Connector deployment.
Segment definition.
Policy alignment.
And ZCC deployment.

Partial deployment—

is partial control.

ZIA alone—

leaves private access exposed.

ZPA alone—

leaves internet traffic uninspected.

Neither is Zero Trust.

> ***Partial deployment is not incremental progress. It is an incomplete security posture.***

This is not an argument against phased implementation—

phased implementation is the responsible approach.

It is an argument that each phase:

must be understood for what it controls—

what it does not.

The organization must know where control does not exist—

at every stage of execution.

ZIA vs. ZPA — Control Plane Summary

Dimension	ZIA	ZPA
Traffic domain	Internet & SaaS (outbound)	Private applications (internal)
OSI layer	Layers 4–7 (inspection)	Layer 7 (proxy/broker)
Primary function	Inspect, filter, protect outbound traffic	Broker least-privilege app access
Network exposure	User exits to internet via ZIA cloud	User never touches the private network
Trust model	Inspect all traffic; enforce policy on content	Verify identity; authorize per application
Key config element	Policies, URL categories, DLP rules	Application Segments, App Connectors
Threat protection	Malware, C2, phishing, DLP	Lateral movement elimination, app isolation
Dependency	ZCC (recommended) or PAC/GRE forwarding	ZCC required for seamless access
Without the other	Internet controlled; private apps ungoverned	Private apps controlled; internet uninspected

Closing Principle

Access is not control.

Reachability is not governance.

Connectivity is not authorization.

Architecture becomes dangerous—
when those ideas are treated as the same.

VPN grants presence.

ZPA grants access.

ZIA governs what leaves.

ZPA governs what is reached.

These are not overlapping functions.

They are different decisions.

And when that distinction is missed—
organizations do not eliminate risk.

They relocate it into the architecture.

Zero Trust does not begin
when a user connects.
It begins—
when access is defined,
enforced,
and contained.

And when that distinction is ignored—
access becomes illusion.

References

1. Cisco Documentation — VPN network-layer behavior and remote access model
2. Zscaler Documentation — ZPA architecture, App Connectors, and Application Segments
3. Zscaler Documentation — ZIA architecture and outbound inspection model
4. NIST SP 800-207 — Zero Trust Architecture principles
5. CISA Zero Trust Maturity Model — application, device, and policy maturity guidance

Chapter 5

When Architecture Becomes Exposure

Architecture is often presented as a solution:

A design.

A blueprint.

A structured method to reduce risk.

And improve control.

But architecture does not eliminate risk.

It distributes it.

And when built on flawed assumptions—

architecture does not protect the organization.

It exposes it.

Architecture does not fail loudly.

It fails quietly,

structurally—

and systemically.

A misconfigured access model

does not produce

a single failure event.

It creates a condition
of recurring, systemic exposure—
one that remains difficult to detect
because the system continues to function
while the vulnerability persists beneath the surface.
This is what makes architectural failure dangerous.

It is not immediately visible.

It is embedded.

When architecture is incorrect:
Risk is not eliminated—
it is redistributed
into the gaps between components.

Exposure is not accidental—
it is a repeatable outcome
of the design.

Failure does not arrive suddenly—
it accumulates
until pressure reveals it.

The problem is not complexity.

The problem is misplaced control.

When organizations misunderstand
where control actually exists,
they build architecture
around the wrong boundaries.

And those boundaries—

become the source of exposure.

5.1 Incomplete Zero Trust: ZIA + ZPA Without ZCC

Zero Trust is often implemented in parts:

ZIA is introduced.

ZPA follows.

And the organization believes—

it has achieved Zero Trust.

In reality—it has not.

Because control is not defined by components.

It is defined by consistency.

ZIA governs internet and SaaS traffic.

ZPA governs private application access.

But neither component governs the endpoint.

And without endpoint-level enforcement—

control becomes conditional:

Applied to some traffic
Under some conditions
Through some paths

> ***Partial Zero Trust does not reduce risk. It redistributes it.***

The Role of ZCC in Unified Enforcement

Enforcement without alignment—
is not enforcement.

It is activity.

Policies exist.
Controls exist.
But they act in isolation—
each one blind to the others.

This is the fragmentation that quietly erodes Zero Trust.

Zscaler Client Connector (ZCC)
is the control layer
that removes it.

Zscaler Client Connector (ZCC)
is the control layer
that removes that fragmentation.

It does not add capability.
It aligns enforcement.

It ensures:
Internet traffic is consistently inspected.
Private application access is consistently brokered.
Device posture is included in access decisions.

Without ZCC

Traffic steering becomes inconsistent.

Internet traffic must be redirected through alternative methods—
such as PAC files or GRE/IPSec tunnels.

These approaches work—
but they are
device-dependent,
harder to standardize,
and lack endpoint awareness.

ZPA access becomes configuration-dependent.

The seamless, always-on access model—
where private applications behave as if they are local—
depends on ZCC.

Without it:
Access requires manual configuration—
or is limited to browser-based access patterns.

Device context disappears from policy.

ZCC provides posture signals:
Operating system.
Patch level.
And certificate state.

Without those signals—
policy cannot evaluate device health.

Access becomes identity-based only.

Enforcement varies by path and condition.

The same user
accessing the same application
from the same device—
can experience different outcomes
depending on how traffic is routed
and how the device is configured

And when enforcement varies—
control breaks.

ZCC is not optional.

It is the mechanism
that makes Zero Trust enforcement
consistent.

And consistency—
is what Zero Trust requires.

What Incomplete Deployment Actually Looks Like

▸Real-World Execution Signal—ZIA + ZPA Without ZCC Pattern

An organization deploys ZIA using PAC files.

ZPA is configured for private application access.

The deployment is declared complete.

Zero Trust is declared achieved.

In reality:

Endpoints without ZCC forward traffic inconsistently.
Some traffic is inspected.
Some bypasses inspection.

ZPA access works—
but requires explicit configuration per device.

Device posture is not part of access decisions.

The organization believes it has Zero Trust. It has partial enforcement—which is architecturally equivalent to a gap.

5.2 When Control Is Fragmented, Exposure Is Inevitable

Control must be continuous.

Not partial.

Not situational.

Not dependent on access method.

When control fragments—

exposure becomes predictable.

Different paths produce different enforcement.

Different users experience different policy outcomes.

Different devices expose different surfaces.

This is not a gap.

It is an open path.

Attackers do not defeat Zero Trust.

They identify where it is not enforced.

How Architectural Gaps Become Attack Paths

Attackers do not target
the strongest control.

They target inconsistency.

Hybrid environments—
where legacy access
and incomplete Zero Trust coexist—
create blind spots.

Traffic that bypasses enforcement:
Generates no signal.
Triggers no policy.
Produces no visibility.

From an attacker's perspective—
that is not a vulnerability.

It is an entry point.

The pattern is simple:
Find the gap.
Enter through it.
Operate where visibility does not exist.

Incomplete Zero Trust does not stop attackers. It redirects them.

5.3 ZCC and PKI — What It Does and What It Does Not Do

Architecture does not fail because technology is missing.

It fails because trust is assumed where it was never established.

Public Key Infrastructure (PKI) defines trust.

It defines:

Which certificates are trusted

How identity is validated

How encrypted traffic can be inspected without breaking integrity

Without PKI, these functions do not disappear.

They become inconsistent.

ZCC enforces that trust at the endpoint:

It ensures traffic is routed through the correct enforcement path.
It carries device posture into every access decision.
It distributes and applies trust anchors on the device.
It executes policy consistently—regardless of network conditions.

ZCC does not define trust.

It makes trust real.

The Misconception

Read enough about Zero Trust online and a quiet assumption begins to surface:

"that Zscaler Client Connector (ZCC)
can replace PKI."
It cannot.

Trust is often confused with enforcement.

That confusion becomes structural
inside Zero Trust architecture—
where one misplaced assumption
can unravel the entire model.

ZCC is not a certificate authority.

It does not establish trust.

PKI remains the source of identity.
ZCC enforces trust—
at the endpoint.

PKI issues and anchors identity.

ZCC validates that identity,
applies policy against it,
and revokes access when posture shifts.

One defines who you are.

The other decides what you can do—right now.

Strip out either one—
and the model collapses.

PKI without enforcement
becomes theoretical.

Enforcement without PKI
becomes arbitrary.

What ZCC Actually Does

ZCC is the agent that sits on the endpoint
and makes Zero Trust operational.

It steers traffic
into ZIA and ZPA.

It reports device posture in real time.

It distributes the trust anchors
required for inspection and policy evaluation.

From that foundation,
the platform delivers
what most organizations associate with Zero Trust:

SSL inspection.

Policy enforcement.

Secure application access.

But notice what just happened.

Every one of those
is an enforcement action—

a decision applied,
a rule executed,
a session inspected.

None of them establish trust.

They operate on it.

PKI establishes identity.

ZCC enforces policy
against that identity.

The distinction matters.

Because enforcement without identity
cannot validate trust.

And identity without enforcement
cannot control access.

ZCC is the operational layer
that makes the model executable.

But it is not the authority
that defines trust itself.

It enforces the architecture.

It does not become the architecture.

What ZCC Does Not Do

Before we credit ZCC with too much,

it is worth naming

what it was never designed to do.

ZCC is often mistaken

for the source of trust itself.

It is not.

Enforcement and trust governance

are not the same function.

ZCC does not issue certificates.

It does not manage certificate lifecycle

or revocation.

It does not establish
enterprise trust hierarchy.

And it does not govern trust centrally.

What it does
is narrower—
and important.

It enables control.

But it does not define trust.

That line is not a limitation.

It is a design boundary.

What Happens Without PKI

The most dangerous condition
inside Zero Trust architecture
is not failure.

It is partial functionality.
Because nothing appears broken.
The system still functions.
Users still connect.
Policies still execute.
Traffic still flows.
But look closer
at the trust model underneath—
and something has changed.

Trust becomes distributed.

Trust becomes implicit.

Trust becomes fragmented.

Zscaler provides the mechanisms
required to keep the system operational—
but operation
is not governance.

The lights stay on.

The authority is gone.

And nothing on the surface
will tell you the difference.

Why This Is Not Equivalent to PKI

Operational capability
is not the same thing
as governed trust maturity.

Systems can function
while trust remains
structurally fragmented.

It is tempting—
to look at a functioning Zscaler deployment
and conclude that PKI
has been quietly replaced.

It has not.

Without enterprise PKI:
Certificate lifecycle
is not centrally governed.

Revocation becomes inconsistent.

Trust cannot be fully audited.

And advanced controls
remain out of reach.

The system works.
But working
is not the same thing
as maturing.
A deployment can operate for years
in this condition—
functional,
defensible on the surface,
and quietly accumulating risk
underneath.

The TPM Reality — Blocker or Gap?

Mature execution
does not confuse functionality
with completeness.

And it does not conceal
architectural gaps
behind operational success.

Lack of PKI
is not a blocker.

Zscaler can operate without it.

That is precisely
what makes the condition dangerous.

Because operational
gets mistaken for complete.

And a gap
that does not prevent deployment
tends to disappear
from the conversation
the moment deployment succeeds.

So, the discipline is this:

Proceed with deployment.

But do not declare completeness.

Define PKI
as a future-state requirement—
explicitly,
in writing,
on the roadmap.

A controlled gap
is acceptable.

An unspoken gap
is not.

What Safe Execution Looks Like

Safe execution
is not the absence
of architectural limitation.

It is the disciplined management of it.

Operating without enterprise PKI
does not mean operating without control.

It means operating
with greater intentionality.

A disciplined deployment includes:
Controlled certificate distribution.
Explicit SSL inspection policies.
Monitoring of trust failures.
Managed certificate usage.
Clear documentation of trust limitations.

None of this closes the PKI gap.

What it does
is contain it—
so, the gap remains known,

bounded,
and visible
to anyone who inherits the environment.

This is not compromise.

It is controlled progression.

What Failure Looks Like

Failure here
is not technical.

It is narrative.

Failure is not
the absence of PKI.

Failure is standing in front of leadership
and declaring:

"We have full Zero Trust."

while operating
without governed trust
underneath.

That is not Zero Trust.

That is partial enforcement
wearing the language of completeness.

ZCC does not replace PKI.

It compensates for its absence—
just enough
to enable enforcement.

But enforcement
without governed trust—
is incomplete by definition.

PKI defines trust.

ZCC enforces it.
When PKI is absent—
trust does not disappear.

It fragments.

Architecture Is Not Neutral

Architecture is often treated
as a backdrop—
a static diagram
behind the real work.

It is not.

Architecture is an active force.

It either reinforces control—
or amplifies exposure.

There is no middle state.

When control is consistent—
architecture protects.

When control is fragmented—
architecture exposes.

Exposure is not accidental.

It is either designed—
or left undefined.

And in architecture,
undefined is a decision.

Organizations rarely lose control suddenly.

They lose it gradually—
through assumptions.

Through partial implementation.

Through incomplete architecture.

Until a real-world execution event
reveals what was actually built.

That is the moment
architecture stops protecting—
and becomes exposure.

Closing Principle

Everything in this chapter
points to a single discipline:
Never confuse what is operating—
with what is governed.

Architecture can appear complete
on paper.

But paper is not perimeter—
the endpoint is.

Enforcement reveals the truth.

ZIA can inspect.

ZPA can broker access.

But without ZCC
on the endpoint—
enforcement is not consistent.

And when enforcement
is not consistent—
control does not hold.

This is the line
the chapter has been drawing
from the beginning:

PKI defines trust.

ZCC enforces it.

Remove either side,
and Zero Trust
is not complete.

It is exposed.

References

1. NIST, Zero Trust Architecture (SP 800-207) — foundational principles of continuous verification and no implicit trust.
2. CISA, Zero Trust Maturity Model v2.0 — device-based enforcement and maturity progression.
3. Zscaler Documentation — ZIA, ZPA, and Client Connector architecture and enforcement model.
4. Zscaler ThreatLabz, State of Zero Trust Transformation (2023) — risks in hybrid and partial Zero Trust environments.
5. Zscaler Documentation — SSL inspection, intermediate CA, and enrollment certificate behavior.

PART III

The Migration Lens

A direct extension of Cloud Migration PM Bible™. Discovery and execution discipline applied to Zero Trust.

Chapter 6

Discovery Before Decision

Most organizations believe they fail during implementation.
They do not.
They fail before it begins.

Execution is not where failure is born.
Execution is where failure becomes visible.

Failure is not introduced during execution.
It is carried into execution—
through incomplete understanding.

The gap between what an organization believes it knows about its environment
and what actually exists—
is where Zero Trust collapses.

This is not a new principle.
In Cloud Migration PM Bible™,
discovery defined how migrations succeed.
Here—
it defines something more consequential:
how Zero Trust survives execution.

The context has changed.
The technology has evolved.
The stakes have increased.

But the truth remains unchanged.

Control does not begin when systems move.

It begins when they are understood.

Because what is not discovered cannot be controlled.

And what is not controlled—

will fail under pressure.

> ***Discovery is not preparation. It is control—before execution begins.***

This is where most Zero Trust programs collapse.

Not because the technology is flawed.

Not because the architecture is wrong.

But because the organization does not fully understand:

what it is trying to protect.

how systems interact with each other.

where dependencies actually exist in the environment.

That gap is not visible in planning.

It becomes visible in execution.

And by then—

it is already too late to address it without disruption.

6.1 Application Discovery as the First Gate of ZPA

ZPA does not tolerate ambiguity.

This is not a product limitation—

it is a design principle.

An application that is not defined—
cannot be accessed.

An access path that is not configured—
does not exist.

Applications must be defined
before ZPA deployment proceeds.

That definition must be complete across four dimensions:

Name — the application identifier used in policy and reporting.
FQDN (Fully Qualified Domain Name) — the DNS name through which the application is addressed and resolved.
IP address or range — for non-DNS-based access.
Port and protocol — the specific ports and protocols the application uses.

If any of these definitions are incomplete—
access will fail.
Not partially.
Completely.

Because ZPA does not estimate,
approximate,
or default to permissive behavior.

ZPA enforces exactly what is defined.
Nothing more.

Anything outside that definition—
is treated as non-existent.
Not suspicious.

Not degraded.

Simply unreachable.

This is where the discovery gap becomes real.

An incomplete application inventory does not delay execution.

It breaks it.

Not because ZPA fails—

but because ZPA is working correctly.

> ***Zero Trust does not break systems. It exposes what was never properly defined.***

Discovery is not a task.

It is a gate.

Nothing proceeds until that gate is cleared.

What "Complete Enough" Means in Practice

Complete enough does not mean perfect.

But incomplete discovery guarantees failure.

Complete enough means:

All applications required by the first wave population are defined in ZPA Application Segments.

All FQDNs and IP ranges used by those applications are verified—not assumed.

All port and protocol requirements are tested—not inferred.

All dependencies of those applications—authentication services, database connections, API endpoints—are included—not discovered later.

Dependencies are where failures occur.

An application may be defined correctly—
but if it depends on:
directory services
certificate authorities
backend APIs

and those are not included—
access fails.

Not predictably.

Unpredictably.

Every dependency is a hidden gate.
And hidden gates become failure points
the moment execution begins.

Because systems rarely fail
at the visible layer.
They fail
where assumptions were never validated.
Discovery must find them—
before execution does.

6.2 VPN vs. ZPA — The Discovery Gap

VPN and ZPA operate on opposite assumptions.
In VPN:
Access comes first
Understanding comes later

Users connect
Reachability is granted

Discovery happens through observation:

Logs
Traffic
User behavior

This creates the illusion of control.

Access works.

But understanding remains incomplete.

ZPA reverses this entirely.

Understanding comes first.

Access follows.

An application must be defined
before it can be reached

There is no implicit reachability.

No network to explore.

No fallback.

> ***VPN hides dependency gaps. ZPA forces them into the open. And what is forced into the open must be resolved.***

This is not a limitation.

It is enforcement.

It is how Zero Trust becomes real.

Discovery Model Comparison:

VPN Discovery Model	ZPA Discovery Model
Access granted at authentication	Access requires prior definition
Network reachability enables application use	Application definition enables access
Discovery happens through observation after access	Discovery must be completed before access
Unknown applications are accessible by default	Unknown applications are inaccessible by design
Dependency gaps are revealed through failure	Dependency gaps are revealed through definition
Inventory is built from usage data over time	Inventory is required before deployment proceeds
Incomplete knowledge produces reduced visibility	Incomplete knowledge produces access failure

VPN tolerates incomplete understanding.

ZPA does not.

That distinction changes
how discovery must be approached,
validated,
and operationalized—
before deployment begins.

6.3 When the Organization Has No Inventory

Most organizations do not have a complete application inventory.

They believe they do.

But belief is not accuracy.

Applications exist beyond documentation:

legacy systems — applications that pre-date current documentation practices and whose architecture is held only in institutional knowledge.

Undocumented internal services — APIs, microservices, and utility applications deployed by development teams without formal CMDB registration.

Shadow IT — cloud services and SaaS applications adopted by business units without IT involvement.

Embedded dependencies — third-party libraries, authentication services, telemetry endpoints, and CDN resources that applications consume but are not considered "applications" in the traditional sense.

Over time,

environments accumulate systems

faster than governance can track them.

Documentation diverges.

Ownership changes.

Institutional knowledge disappears.

But the dependencies remain.

Some are known.

Some are assumed.

Some are invisible—
until they fail.

> ***An incomplete inventory is not a gap. It is a false sense of control. And false control is more dangerous than acknowledged uncertainty.***

Because it allows execution to proceed—
on the wrong assumption.

When failure occurs—
it is misdiagnosed as a platform issue.

But it is not.

It is a discovery failure.

6.4 Reconstructing Discovery from Operational Data

When discovery is incomplete—
it must be rebuilt.

Not through assumptions—
through evidence.

Documentation reflects intention.

Operational telemetry reflects behavior.

And in complex environments—
behavior is the truth

architecture must eventually answer to.

Enterprise systems continuously generate signals.

Those signals reveal reality:

VPN logs show actual access behavior.
Firewall logs show internal dependencies.
DNS logs expose real application endpoints.
SIEM correlation reveals relationships.
No single source is complete.

> ***Discovery does not need to be perfect. It must be sufficient. Execution does not require certainty. It requires sufficient clarity.***

Sufficient clarity means the organization can define:
What must be reached.
What must be protected.
What must remain inaccessible.
And what dependencies must be preserved for the service to function.

Anything less
is not discovery—
It is hope disguised as planning.

6.5 Application Mapping and Segmentation Strategy

Once applications are discovered,
they must be structured.
Not individually—
but logically.

Discovery identifies applications.
Segmentation makes them controllable.

Applications do not operate in isolation.

They operate in groups.

ZPA reflects that through Application Segments.

Segmentation is not merely
a method of organization.

It is how exposure boundaries
are deliberately constrained
before failure occurs.

Segmentation must be structured by:
Function.
Dependency.
And by access pattern.

This enables:
Policy consistency.
Operational scalability.
And containment.

Containment is the priority.

If a policy fails—
segmentation limits exposure.

Without it—
failure expands.

Segmentation is not organization.

It is control.

Segmentation and Execution

Segmentation defines how migration happens.

Well-structured segments become:

Testable units
Rollback boundaries
And accountable scopes

Poor segmentation creates:

Operational friction
Policy complexity
And execution instability

Segmentation is not just security design.

It is deployment structure.

When segments are clean,
execution can be sequenced.
When segments are confused,
execution inherits confusion.

Discovery Is Not a Phase

Discovery is not a phase in the plan.
It is a condition.

A condition that determines:
Whether execution succeeds—
or fails under pressure.
Organizations that rush discovery do not accelerate.

They destabilize.

Because what they do not understand—
will surface later.

And in Zero Trust—
nothing surfaces quietly.

You cannot secure what you do not understand.

References

1. Zscaler ZPA Documentation — Application Segments & App Connectors
2. Netskope Cloud & Threat Report — Shadow IT and application visibility
3. NIST SP 800-207 — Zero Trust Architecture principles
4. CISA Zero Trust Maturity Model — Application discovery and segmentation
5. Splunk / SIEM Practices — Correlation for dependency mapping

Chapter 7

Migration Is Not Replacement

The danger of "rip and replace" thinking

Modernization vs. forced transition.

Execution requires coexistence—
not disruption.

There is a moment in every transformation
where the wrong decision is made—
not because of poor intent,
not because of lack of knowledge,
not because of lack of capability—
but because of how the problem is framed.

Zscaler is often introduced as a replacement.
A replacement for VPN.
A replacement for legacy security controls.
A replacement for how access has always been delivered.

That framing is where failure begins.

Because enterprise environments are not designed to be replaced.
They are designed to operate—
continuously.

Anything that disrupts that continuity—
becomes a risk to the business.

> *Migration is not replacement.*
> *It is controlled coexistence—until control is proven.*

7.1 The Illusion of "Rip and Replace"

Why simplicity is appealing. Why simplicity creates risk.

"Let's replace it."
It sounds decisive.
It sounds efficient.

It sounds like progress.

It is none of those things.

In enterprise environments, replacement ignores:
Undocumented dependencies
Legacy system behavior under real load

Operational workflows built overtime—
Around current latency,
current routing,
current failure modes,
and user access patterns
that have evolved over years.

embedded trust relationships—
including IP-allowlisted integrations,
certificate-pinned applications,
and source-IP-bound third-party services.

What appears to be a clean transition—
is, in reality,
a disruption
of multiple invisible systems.

Those systems do not fail quietly.
They fail under pressure.

Replacement assumes understanding.
Migration reveals the lack of it.

The pull toward "rip and replace" is not technical—
it is psychological.

When a system is perceived as a source of risk—
the instinct is to remove it immediately.

VPN is not broken.
It is operationally effective—
within the architecture it was designed for.

In environments where systems are primarily internal,
where network boundaries are controlled,
and where access patterns are predictable—
VPN provides reliable connectivity.

It generally extends
network-layer reachability—
through secure remote-access tunnels
that place users inside the environment.

That model works.

But it introduces a condition:
Access is granted at the network level
before it is constrained at the application level.

Once inside—
movement is no longer tightly controlled.

This is not failure.
It is exposure.

And that exposure—
is what drives the urgency to replace it.

But urgency is not control.

In cloud-first environments—
where applications are distributed,
SaaS-driven,
and externally accessible—
network-based access becomes less relevant.

In hybrid environments—
where on-premises systems,
legacy applications,
and modern services coexist—
the decision is not determined
by where the data resides.

An application does not require VPN
merely because it remains
inside an enterprise data center.

On-premises location alone does not justify VPN—
The access requirement does.

Many on-premises private applications
can be accessed through ZPA,
an identity-aware proxy,
VDI,
a privileged-access gateway,
an API gateway,
or a protocol-specific broker.

Traditional VPN or another
tightly controlled network-access mechanism

may remain necessary
when the workflow genuinely requires:

dynamic IP-level connectivity;
unpredictable ports or destinations;
broadcast or multicast behavior;
network discovery;
certain administrative protocols;
site-to-site integration;
legacy name-resolution behavior;
operational technology;
specialized equipment;
or applications whose dependencies
cannot yet be represented
as stable destinations, ports, and protocols.

Even in those circumstances—
VPN should not automatically provide
broad network membership.

Access should be restricted
by identity,
device posture,
destination,
protocol,
time,
segmentation,
and continuous monitoring.

ZPA operates differently.

It provides application-centric,
policy-brokered access—
granting access to authorized
private application destinations
rather than to the broader network itself.

These are not always competing models.
They are different control mechanisms—
selected according to
the actual technical requirement.

The failure occurs when one is removed
without understanding what the other does not replace.

Simplicity is not the problem.

Misunderstood simplicity is.

There are two forms of simplicity in execution:

Simplicity that is engineered—
where complexity is understood, reduced, and controlled.

And simplicity that is assumed—
where complexity is ignored, compressed, and left unresolved.

One reduces risk.

The other hides it.

And what is hidden—

emerges under pressure.

7.2 Why Zscaler Cannot Be Introduced as a Cutover Event

Zero Trust is not a switch. Access models cannot be flipped instantly.

Zscaler does not change tools.

It changes control.

That change is structural:

network-based access → application-based access
implicit trust → explicit verification
connectivity → controlled reachability

These shifts cannot be introduced in a single moment.

Because readiness is never uniform:

Across users
Across applications
Across endpoints
Across identity systems

A cutover assumes alignment.

Enterprise environments rarely provide it.

Zero Trust is not deployed.

It is transitioned into.

As established in discovery:

access in ZPA requires prior definition.

An application that is not defined
cannot be accessed.

But definition is not a label.

It is precision.

In ZPA, applications must be defined using:

Fully qualified domain names (FQDN).
Wildcard domains,
or IP ranges.

Each of these represents a different level of control.

An FQDN defines a single, explicit destination.

It aligns access to how modern applications are actually consumed.

A wildcard domain expands that scope.
It allows access to multiple subdomains—
but reduces precision.

An IP range defines access at the network level.
It is often required for legacy systems—
but it reintroduces broader reach than intended.

This is where most implementations fail.

They define access too broadly—
to make it "work."

And in doing so—
they recreate the very condition Zero Trust was designed to eliminate.

Precision is not optional.
It is the control boundary.

A dependency that is not discovered
will not be defined.

And what is not defined—
will fail during execution.

This is why cutover models collapse.

They assume understanding
that has not yet been proven.

7.3 Coexistence as a Control Strategy

Running legacy and modern access models in parallel. Maintaining continuity during transition.

Coexistence is not compromise.

It is control.

During transition, multiple states must exist:
Legacy VPN remains operational for unmigrated users and applications.
ZPA is introduced in controlled segments tied to discovery scope
User populations move in phases governed by wave criteria.
Applications transition gradually, often beginning with FQDN-defined low-risk targets and progressing toward IP-bound or pinned applications.

This overlap is intentional.

It enables:
Validation before exposure.
Rollback without disruption.
Comparison between access models—
(does ZPA reach what VPN reached,
with the latency the user expected?)
Controlled dependency resolution—
as hidden dependencies surface.

Coexistence protects continuity.

And continuity is what allows control
to exist during change.

Execution reality

Applications do not behave uniformly.

Some are cleanly defined by FQDN.

Others rely on:

Multiple subdomains.
Dynamic endpoints.
And backend service calls.

These often require wildcard definitions—
which expand access beyond a single boundary.

Some applications cannot be defined by domain at all.

They rely on:

Static IP addresses.
IP ranges.
Network-level communication.

These are not exceptions.

They are enterprise reality.

This is where coexistence becomes necessary.

Because ZPA brokers access
at the application level—
while many legacy behaviors still depend
on general network-layer reachability.

During transition:

FQDN-defined applications move first.
Wildcard-defined applications require validation.
IP-based applications require architectural decisions.

Not all applications move at the same pace.

And not all should.

Coexistence allows each to be evaluated—

before it is enforced.

Zscaler Client Connector enables this control:

traffic can be steered
bypassed
or enforced selectively

Not as a workaround—

but as a transition mechanism.

This is where execution becomes real.

Because what was defined in discovery—

is now tested under live conditions.

And what fails here—

was never fully understood before.

Coexistence does not slow execution.

It prevents failure from becoming disruption.

7.4 The Cost of Premature Decommissioning

Why removing legacy too early creates instability.

There is always pressure to remove the old system quickly.

To reduce cost.

To simplify operations.

To declare completion.

That pressure introduces risk.

Premature decommissioning removes:

Fallback access paths

Known operational baselines (the latency, behavior, and failure modes users have adapted to)

Recovery options (the ability to revert without rebuilding)

Forensic continuity (the ability to compare current behavior to a known prior state)

And replaces them with:

Untested dependencies.

Incomplete policies.

Partial visibility.

And no path back

Everything appears stable—

until a condition fails.

Without a fallback—

that failure becomes an outage.

This pattern is consistent across enterprise programs:

The first wave succeeds

The second wave stabilizes

Third wave execution completes

The program is declared successful

Legacy system is removed

And weeks later—

an edge-case integration fails.

A partner gateway.
A scheduled batch job.
A regulatory file transfer.

Something no one owned during transition.

And the system that would have caught it—

no longer exists.

Programs rarely fail during rollout.

They fail after removal.

> *Decommissioning is not a milestone.*
>
> *It is a decision earned through stability.*

7.5 Designing the Transition Model

From legacy to Zero Trust through controlled progression.

A successful Zscaler program is not defined by deployment.

It is defined by transition.

That transition must be structured.

It is not a movement of technology.

It is a controlled shift of behavior, access, and enforcement.

That structure includes:

Phased user migration — aligned to wave progression and readiness.
Application segmentation — translating discovery into enforceable access boundaries.
Dual-access validation — ensuring the same application works across both legacy and ZPA paths.
Policy refinement — adjusting access based on observed behavior, not assumed design.
Controlled decommissioning — defined, measurable, and enforced.

Each phase answers a single question:

Can the new control model fully replace the old—

for this scope?

If the answer is not proven—

the transition does not advance.

This is not hesitation.

It is discipline.

Coexistence introduces operational pressure:

Two access models
Two enforcement paths
Two sets of expectations

That pressure must have an end condition.

A transition model without a defined exit—

is not a transition.

It becomes permanent coexistence.

And permanent coexistence—

is cost without control.

Skipping validation does not accelerate execution.

It shifts risk forward—

into production.

7.6 Control Before Removal

When is it safe to eliminate legacy systems?

Legacy systems are not removed because a new system exists.

They are removed because control has been proven.

That proof must demonstrate:

complete access coverage — every user, every application, every integration migrated or intentionally retired

consistent policy enforcement — the same access decision under the same condition, repeatedly)

stable user experience — latency, MFA cadence, application responsiveness within acceptable bounds

operational support readiness — service teams capable of resolving incidents without falling back to legacy paths

observability completeness — logs, alerts, and ZDX telemetry validated end-to-end)

Only then—

can legacy systems be retired.

Not before.

The question to ask before any decommissioning decision is not—

"Is the new system working?"

The question is—

"If the new system fails right now, what is our next move?"

If the answer requires the legacy system, the legacy system stays.

Dashboards do not prove control.

Behavior does.

Control must be:

Repeatable
Observable
Supportable

Before removal is even considered.

Decommissioning based on visibility alone—
is assumption.

Decommissioning based on proven behavior—
is control.

Closing Principle

Migration is not about replacing systems.

It is about transferring control—
without losing stability.

Zscaler does not succeed because it is deployed.

It succeeds when access is precisely defined,
when behavior aligns with that definition,
and when enforcement holds under real conditions.

FQDN, wildcard domains, and IP ranges
are not configuration details.

They are the boundaries of control.

Define them loosely—
and exposure returns.

Define them precisely—
and control becomes real.

Coexistence is not a delay.

It is the mechanism that allows control to be proven
before it is enforced.

Remove legacy too early—
and you remove the only reference point
that proves the system is working.

Decommissioning is not scheduled.

It is earned.

Control is not declared
because a system is live.

It is demonstrated
through repeatable behavior,
validated outcomes,
and the absence of failure under pressure.

Organizations that attempt replacement:

Move too quickly
Define too broadly
Remove too early

Organizations that succeed in migration:

Discover completely
Define precisely

Validate continuously
And remove only when control is proven

Replacement creates disruption.

Migration preserves control.

And in enterprise environments—
control is not a milestone.

It is the condition that must hold
long after deployment is complete.

References

1. Zscaler ThreatLabz. 2024 VPN Risk Report. Survey of over 600 IT, security, and networking professionals. zscaler.com/campaign/threatlabz-vpn-risk-report. Key findings: 56% experienced VPN-related cyberattacks in the prior year; 91% expressed concern about VPN security; 53% of breached enterprises reported lateral movement; 92% concerned about third-party VPN access.
2. Microsoft Learn. Configure Microsoft and Zscaler for a Unified SASE Solution — Coexistence Guidance. learn.microsoft.com/entra/global-secure-access/how-to-zscaler-coexistence. Documents Zscaler Client Connector forwarding profiles, app profile bypass lists, and FQDN/IP exemption configuration required for stack coexistence.
3. Zscaler. Source IP Anchoring — Innovations Page and Configuring Source IP Anchoring — ZIA Help Portal. zscaler.com/innovations/source-ip-anchoring; help.zscaler.com/zia/configuring-source-ip-anchoring. Mechanism for preserving source-IP-dependent integrations during VPN-to-ZPA transition.

Chapter 8

The Seven Phases Applied to Zero Trust

The Technical Project Manager's Execution Playbook

Translating migration discipline into Zscaler program delivery—
from theory to operational control.

There comes a point in every transformation
where understanding is no longer enough.

The architecture may be correct.
The platform may be capable.
The design may even be aligned.

And still—
the implementation fails.

Not because the technology was wrong.

But because execution was not controlled.

This is not a new pattern.

It reflects a principle established in Cloud Migration PM Bible™:
Execution is where strategy is tested—
and where most programs fail.

Zscaler does not change that truth.

It intensifies it.

Zero Trust removes tolerance.

It does not allow ambiguity to remain hidden inside the network.

It forces precision.
And precision—
under pressure—
requires discipline.

This chapter is not about what Zscaler is.

It is about how to run it:
As a program
As a transformation
And as a controlled execution model that must survive real-world conditions

The seven phases that follow are not a theoretical sequence.

They are operational control points.

Miss one—
and risk is absorbed into the program.

Ignore one—
and instability becomes inevitable.

These phases have a direct correlation to successful Zscaler implementation—
when control is enforced with them.

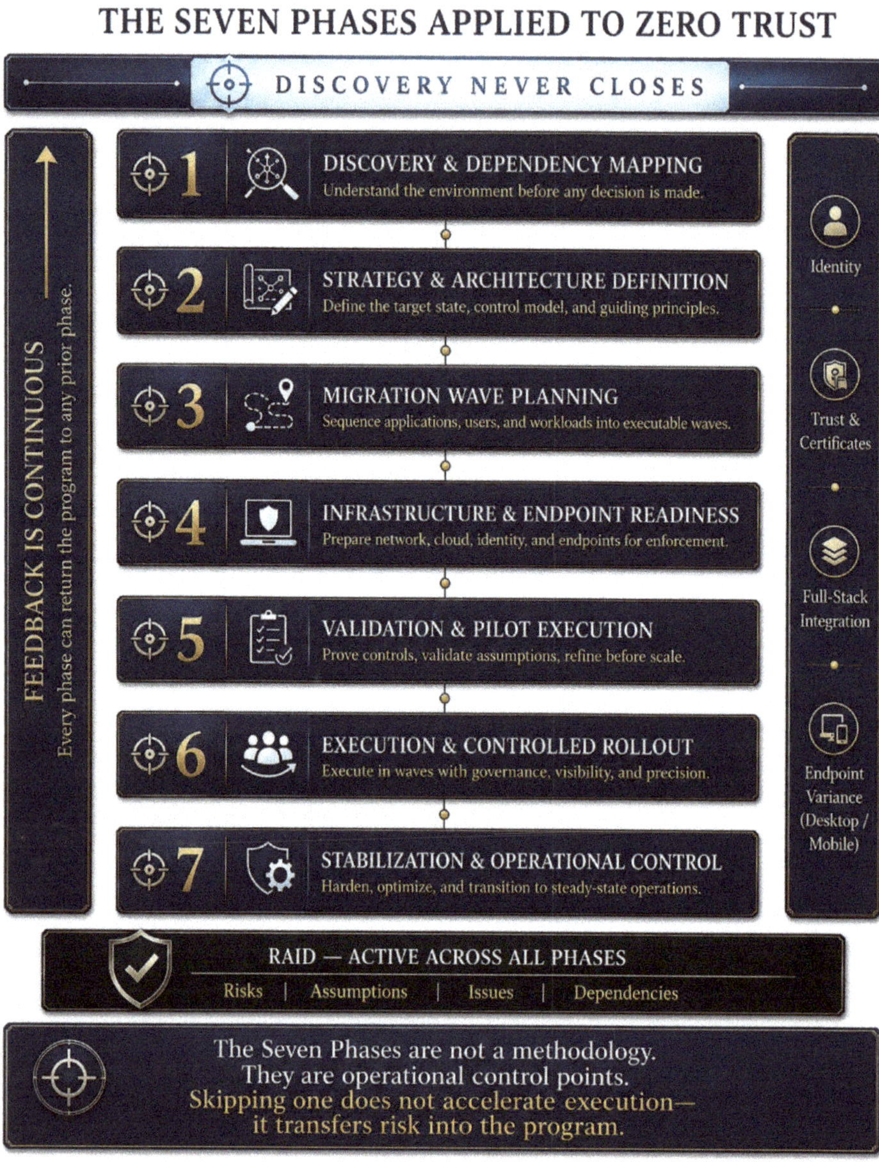

Figure 8.1 The Seven Phases Applied to Zero Trust — Control Architecture and Cross-Cutting Disciplines.

These phases alone do not guarantee success—
discipline does.

8.1 Phase 1 — Discovery & Dependency Mapping

Application inventory and validation. Identity and access dependencies. Network and traffic flow analysis.

Discovery determines whether execution is survivable.

A foundational principle, established in Cloud Migration PM Bible™, remains unchanged:

Discovery is not preparation.

It is control—

before execution begins.

ZPA enforces that reality.

Access cannot be broadly granted and refined later.

It must be explicitly defined by application;

FQDN, wildcard domain, or addressable

IP range;

ports and protocols;

and the segment group that governs policy.

In the ZPA model, an application segment is

the atomic unit of access.

This is not a configuration preference.

It is a structural decision.

FQDN-based definitions align access to how applications are consumed.

They survive infrastructure changes, IP shifts, and cloud migration without rewriting policy.

Wildcard domains expand access.

They introduce flexibility—but reduce precision.

IP ranges enable legacy access.

But they reintroduce broader exposure.

Definition is not a label.

It is precision.

Discovery must therefore produce:

A validated application inventory.

Ownership mapping—business and technical.

Dependency chains—North-South and East-West.

Identity alignment—which IdP groups consume which apps.

Segmentation candidates—logical grouping for segment groups.

And a defined set of unknowns—every system that cannot be classified yet.

The unknowns matter more than the inventory.

Every program produces a list of what it understands.

Few produce a disciplined list of what it does not.

And it is the second list—
not the first—
that determines outcome.

Because in Zero Trust,
an unclassified application is not absent.

It is unprotected.

When discovery is incomplete—
execution inherits that uncertainty.

And uncertainty does not remain hidden.

It surfaces—

under pressure.

8.2 Phase 2 — Strategy & Architecture Definition

ZIA vs. ZPA vs. hybrid approach. Access model design (application vs. network). Segmentation and policy architecture.

Strategy creates alignment.

Execution reveals its strength.

Zscaler introduces a structural shift in how access is governed:

Network-based access → Application-based access

Implicit trust → Explicit verification

Connectivity → Controlled reachability

ZIA governs internet and SaaS traffic—

secure web gateway, DLP, sandboxing, SSL inspection.

ZPA governs private application access—

broker-mediated, identity-bound, least-privilege.

ZCC (Zscaler Client Connector) enforces both

at the endpoint, forwarding traffic based on policy.

This is not product separation.

It is a control model.

These are not new questions.

They were introduced earlier—

as principles.

Here—
they become architectural decisions.

Each layer answers a different question:
What is leaving the organization—and is it safe?
Who is reaching what private resource—and are they entitled?
Is the device trusted, in the right state, taking the right path?

Clarity must exist at the strategy stage.

Because once execution begins—
those decisions are no longer theoretical.

The program must determine:
Which traffic transitions first—
typically, internet egress before private access.

What remains hybrid during transition—
and why.

Where full client enforcement is required—
and where browser-based access is sufficient.

Clientless access is not a convenience.
It is a deliberate control decision.

For third parties,
for BYOD populations,
for unmanaged devices—
ZPA can broker access without deploying an agent.

That expands reach.

But it also removes layers of enforcement
that would otherwise exist at the endpoint.

This is not a limitation.
It is a tradeoff.
And that tradeoff must be understood—
before it is deployed.

The strategy must also define:
Which existing controls remain during transition.

Which are reduced—
and which are removed entirely.

Not as a future decision—
but as part of the architecture itself.

Segmentation must be operational.

Not aspirational.

Because in ZPA—
segmentation is not design.
It is enforcement.

Application segments define:
Who receives access.
What they can reach.
And under which conditions that access is allowed:
Identity.

Posture.

Location.

Risk.

All converge at that boundary.

Architecture often appears correct in design.
Its integrity is revealed only in execution.

And segmentation that cannot be governed—
cannot be enforced.

8.3 Phase 3 — Migration Wave Planning

User segmentation (IT, pilot, business units). Application grouping and sequencing. Risk-based wave execution strategy.

There is no responsible single-motion deployment.
A core execution principle—
reinforced from Cloud Migration PM Bible™.
Phased execution is not caution.
It is control.
Wave planning defines survivability.

A structured rollout considers:
User maturity (technical literacy, change tolerance).
Application risk (criticality, blast radius if access fails).
Dependency density (how many systems depend on this one).
Business tolerance (operational windows, peak periods).
Endpoint variation (managed vs. unmanaged, OS mix, BYOD posture).

Typical sequencing:

Wave 0 — Engineering and platform validation (the program team itself).

Wave 1 — IT pilot (technical users with high tolerance and diagnostic capability).

Wave 2 — Low-risk business users (single-application profiles).

Wave 3 — Core business operations (revenue-generating, customer-facing).

Wave 4 — Edge cases, exceptions, and high-friction populations (executives, M&A entities, OT environments, third parties).

Pilot success creates confidence.

But:

A successful pilot proves possibility.

It does not prove enterprise readiness.

Pilots run with attentive participants, fresh agents, and engaged support.

Enterprise scale runs with distracted users, drifted endpoints, and overloaded service desks.

The wave model exists precisely to surface that gap before it becomes an incident.

Every wave must carry its own rollback.

Not as documentation—
but as a rehearsed, observable operation.

A rollback that has not been simulated before a wave begins is not a rollback.

It is a hope.

And hope is not a control.

8.4 Phase 4 — Infrastructure & Endpoint Readiness

ZCC deployment strategy (desktop and mobile endpoints). Certificate readiness and PKI alignment. Identity provider integration and validation.

Programs often become unstable at this phase—
quietly.
Endpoints are not uniform.
ZCC must be deployed as a controlled mechanism—
not a generic agent rollout.

Readiness includes:
Endpoint deployment model (MDM, GPO, package manager, manual).
Identity integration (SAML/OIDC binding to the chosen IdP).
Certificate trust (root and intermediate distribution to OS and application trust stores).
Inspection strategy (which categories, which exemptions, which user groups).
Policy mapping (forwarding profiles, app profiles, posture profiles).

Certificate strategy is not secondary.

Trust without inspection—
removes visibility.
Control requires deliberate balance.

And certain traffic (banking, healthcare,
certificate-pinned mobile applications)
must be deliberately exempted from inspection by policy—
not accidentally discovered in production.

Readiness is not measured in coverage.

It is measured in predictability.

A 95% deployment is not a 95% success.

It is a 5% incident surface—
waiting to be discovered by the users least equipped to absorb it.

The endpoints that fail are rarely the ones that were planned for.

They are the contractors, the executives, the field operators, the shared kiosks—

the populations that were assumed to be edge cases

until they became the program's most visible failure.

Readiness must therefore include:

A deployment posture report (per OS, per management framework, per user population).

A tested removal path (because what cannot be uninstalled cannot be governed).

A coexistence model for legacy VPN, EDR, and other agents already on the endpoint.

A defined behavior for offline, captive-portal, and constrained-network conditions.

And a service-desk runbook that exists before the first ticket arrives.

Endpoint readiness is not a milestone.

It is the difference between a program that scales—

and a program that retreats.

8.5 Phase 5 — Validation & Pilot Execution

Controlled pilot groups. Policy validation and traffic behavior. Experience validation.

Validation is not connectivity.

It is control verification.

Another principle carried forward:

Validation does not confirm success.

It exposes failure—

before scale.

Validation must confirm:

Correct access behavior (entitled users reach entitled apps).

Correct denial behavior (unentitled users are blocked, and the block is observable).

Policy enforcement accuracy (the rule that fired is the rule that was intended).

Traffic path integrity (Client Connector → Service Edge → App Connector → application).

Acceptable user experience (latency, MFA prompt cadence, application responsiveness).

Observability completeness (logs reach the SIEM, alerts route correctly, ZDX data is usable).

What works in isolation—

may not survive at scale.

A pilot must include at least one negative test per critical policy.

A policy that has only ever been observed allowing traffic has not been validated.

It has been assumed.

Every pilot must define its exit before it begins.

Not as a date—

but as a set of observable conditions.

Without defined exit criteria, a pilot does not end.

It dissolves.

And a pilot that dissolves never produces the evidence required to authorize scale.

8.6 Phase 6 — Execution & Controlled Rollout

Wave-based deployment. Live enforcement and monitoring. Cross-functional coordination.

Execution is where all prior discipline is tested.

This is not deployment.

It is controlled change under pressure.

The program must manage:

Rollout cadence (per wave, per region, per business unit).

Stakeholder alignment (executive sponsorship, business owners, service desk).

Issue triage (severity classification, ownership assignment, time-to-acknowledge).

Escalation paths (technical, operational, executive).

Communication (proactive, scheduled, transparent—not reactive).

Rollback readiness (per-user, per-segment, per-policy—and rehearsed).

The defining factor is not speed.
It is control.

A rollout that moves slower
but holds its commitments
outperforms a rollout
that moves fast and creates incidents—
every time,
in every program,
without exception.

Execution has a tempo.

And tempo is not pace.

Pace is how fast users are migrated.

Tempo is how reliably the program closes the loop—
between change introduced,
signal observed,
and decision made.

A program that introduces change faster than it can interpret signal
is not executing.

It is accumulating risk.

8.7 Phase 7 — Stabilization & Operational Control

Post-deployment monitoring. Incident response. Transition to operations.

Deployment is not completion.

A principle reinforced through prior work:
Completion is not when systems move.
It is when they stabilize.

Stabilization includes:
Hypercare (defined duration, defined exit criteria, defined ownership).
Monitoring (ZDX, SIEM, ITSM integration verified end-to-end).
Issue trend analysis (repeat incidents indicate design gaps, not user error).
Policy tuning (least-privilege refined based on observed access, not predicted access).
Ownership transition (program → operations, with documented runbooks and on-call coverage).
The system must demonstrate:
Consistent control under load.
Stable user experience across geographies and device types.
Operational ownership that does not depend on the program team.

Most programs do not fail at deployment.

They fail at the handoff.

Hypercare is not a holding period.

It is a controlled transfer of accountability.
And accountability does not transfer through documentation alone.

It transfers through:

Operational shadowing (operations works tickets with the program team, not after them).

On-call rotation alignment (operations carries the pager before the program team departs).

Runbook validation (every documented procedure executed once, by the team that will own it).

Knowledge transfer that is observable—not assumed.

A program that exits hypercare on a calendar date
has not transitioned.

It has abandoned.

Stabilization is complete
when operations can carry the system forward—
without the program team in the room.

Only then—
is the program complete.

8.8 Full-Stack Zscaler Implementation Model

ZIA — Internet and SaaS control. ZPA — Private application access. ZCC — Endpoint enforcement. ZDX — Observability.

Zscaler operates as a unified control stack—
not as isolated components.

The stack must therefore be understood in layers:

Enforcement Layer — ZIA and ZPA define internet, SaaS, and private application control.

Endpoint Layer — ZCC applies forwarding, posture, and traffic-steering behavior at the endpoint.

Observability Laye — ZDX provides telemetry, user-experience monitoring, path visibility, and operational insight across the environment.

ZDX does not enforce access.

It validates whether the system is operating correctly under real-world conditions.

Enforcement without observability is not control.

It is configuration.

Layer	Governs	Primary control surface
ZIA	Outbound internet and SaaS	URL/category, SSL inspection, DLP, sandboxing
ZPA	Inbound to private apps	Application segments, access policies, posture
ZCC	The endpoint itself	Forwarding profile, app profile, posture profile
ZDX	Operational visibility	Path analytics, user experience, telemetry, incident correlation

Each layer reinforces the others.

Remove ZIA—
and outbound risk goes uninspected.

Remove ZPA—

and private access reverts to network exposure.

Remove ZCC—

and enforcement becomes inconsistent across off-network conditions.

Remove ZDX—

and the program becomes blind to whether any of it is working.

The program must be designed against the full stack—
even if implementation sequences only one layer at a time.

8.9 Identity, Policy, and Access Integration

Identity as the foundation of access precision.

Identity is foundational.

Access precision is determined by identity accuracy.
If inaccurate—
control collapses.

Policy must align with:
Identity attributes (department, role, location, employment status).
Group structures (used as the primary policy subject).
Lifecycle governance (joiner, mover, leaver — automated, not manual).

The organization must establish a single authoritative identity source before execution begins.
Whether the environment uses Microsoft Entra ID, Okta, or another identity provider—
policy alignment depends on identity consistency.

Two sources of truth produce two sources of access.

And two sources of access produce drift.

Drift is not visible in design.

It is visible only when revocation is required—

and cannot be executed.

Direct assignment of administrative access outside governed group structures introduces instability into the control model.

Joiner, mover, and leaver processes must therefore be automated, validated, and continuously governed.

A real-world failure pattern appears when administrative access can be granted—

but cannot be reliably revoked.

That condition transforms identity into a single point of failure.

Zero Trust is not defined by how access is granted.

It is defined by how precisely and reliably that access can be removed.

Without identity discipline—

Zero Trust becomes theoretical.

The IdP is not a dependency of the Zscaler program.

It is part of the Zscaler program.

8.10 Certificate, Trust, and Secure Communication

Designing trust deliberately, not discovering it during execution.

Trust must be designed.

Not assumed.

Certificate strategy defines:

Visibility (what can be inspected).

Inspection capability (how deeply, on what traffic).

Application compatibility (what must be exempted, and why).

Governance (who owns the signing authority, how rotation occurs, how revocation is handled).

It must be designed—
not discovered during execution.

A Zscaler implementation without a deliberate
certificate strategy will, in production, exhibit
the same symptom in three different forms:
silent breakage of pinned applications;
certificate warnings on developer workstations;
inspection blind spots that are not visible until an audit.

All three are preventable in design.
Certificate pinning is not an operational surprise.

It is a known architectural condition—
that must be accounted for before deployment.

Certificate governance must also define:
How trust stores are distributed across desktop and mobile endpoints.
How certificate rotation is communicated—to operations, to application owners, and to the service desk.
How inspection exceptions are documented, reviewed, and approved.
How exceptions expire—because an exception without an expiration is a permanent gap.

Certificate strategy is not a security artifact.

It is an execution constraint.

And like every constraint in this chapter—
it is cheaper in design
than in production.

8.11 Endpoint Strategy — Desktop vs. Mobile

Why mobile requires a distinct execution model.

Mobile is not a reduced version of desktop.
It is a different execution environment.

Desktop endpoints — Windows, macOS, and Linux — generally provide:
Full administrative control through MDM, GPO, or enterprise management tooling.
More consistent enforcement of forwarding profiles.
More predictable certificate distribution across OS and application trust stores.
More stable tunnel persistence and background execution behavior.

Mobile endpoints — iOS, iPadOS, Android, and ChromeOS — operate differently. They rely more heavily on operating-system-controlled networking behavior, constrained enforcement paths, and mobile management posture.

That includes:
Per-app VPN models and system-extension limits.
Certificate, profile, and Zscaler Client Connector delivery through MDM.
Background activity and battery-management controls that can affect tunnel uptime.
Platform-specific variation between iOS, which is more tightly controlled, and Android, which is more flexible but more variable across vendors.
These differences directly affect:
Traffic steering decisions.
Policy enforcement consistency.
Certificate trust behavior.
User experience.

Deployment strategy and rollout timing.

Mobile introduces additional constraints that cannot be treated as desktop afterthoughts.

Those include:
Which applications are included or excluded from per-app VPN behavior.
How always-on tunnel restrictions behave by platform.
How re-authentication frequency is affected by background process limits.
How trust is handled when mobile certificate behavior differs from desktop trust models.

For that reason,
mobile must be treated
as a dedicated rollout strategy—
not as an extension of desktop deployment.

Mobile therefore requires its own pilot path,
its own support readiness model,
and its own rollback criteria—
validated independently from desktop execution.

A program that schedules mobile
as the final task of a desktop wave
will usually discover,
after cutover,
that the mobile rollout is—
its own program:
under-scoped
under-resourced
and now urgent

8.12 Observability and Operational Telemetry

ZDX, SIEM, and ITSM integration. The instrumentation that makes control visible.

A control that cannot be observed is not a control.

It is a configuration.

Zscaler enforces.

ZDX explains.

SIEM correlates.

ITSM responds.

If any of those four loops is missing—

the program will detect failure later than its users.

And in Zero Trust,

late detection is operationally indistinguishable

from no detection.

Observability must therefore deliver:

User-experience telemetry (latency, page load, application responsiveness — measured from the endpoint, not from the data center).

Path visibility (Client Connector → Service Edge → App Connector → application — segment by segment, hop by hop).

Policy attribution (which rule fired, for which identity, on which application, at which time).

Security signal (SIEM ingestion of access events, denials, anomalies, and posture changes).

Operational signal (ITSM ticket correlation, repeat-incident detection, hypercare evidence).

Observability is not a dashboard.

It is the discipline of knowing, in real time:

What the system is doing.

Whether that is what it was designed to do.

And where it is drifting from intent.

A program that cannot answer those three questions cannot defend its rollout to operations.

And cannot defend its design to audit.

Enforcement proves capability.

Observability proves control.

Closing Principle

Zscaler does not fail because it is misunderstood.

It fails because it is executed without structure.

The architecture can be correct.

The platform can be capable.

The policies can be defined.

And still—
the implementation fails.

Because execution was not controlled.

This is not unique to Zscaler.

It is the same pattern established in Cloud Migration PM Bible™.

Execution is where strategy is tested—
and where most programs collapse.

Zscaler intensifies that reality.

Because Zero Trust does not tolerate ambiguity.

It exposes it.

Every gap in discovery becomes an access failure.

Every imprecise definition becomes exposure.

Every missed dependency becomes an incident.
Immediately.
The Seven Phases are not a methodology.

They are a control system.

Discovery defines reality.

Strategy defines behavior.

Waves control movement.

Readiness determines stability.

Validation exposes failure.

Execution enforces change.

Stabilization proves control.

Miss one—
and risk is absorbed.

Ignore one—
and failure becomes inevitable.

A Zscaler implementation does not succeed
when access works.

It succeeds when:
Access is precisely defined.
Behavior aligns with that definition.
And enforcement holds under real conditions.

This is not configuration.

It is discipline.

This chapter does not describe how Zscaler works.

It defines how Zscaler survives.

And survival—
is determined entirely by execution.

References

1. Zscaler. Zero Trust User-to-App Segmentation with ZPA — Reference Architecture. zscaler.com/resources/reference-architectures.
2. Zscaler. Configuring Application Discovery — ZPA Admin Portal. help.zscaler.com/zpa.
3. Zscaler. Zscaler Client Connector — Platform Overview. zscaler.com/platform/zscaler-client-connector.
4. Zscaler. Third-Party Access and BYOD Security with ZTNA. zscaler.com/products-and-solutions/byod-with-ztna.
5. Zscaler. Zscaler Client Connector — Supported Operating Systems. help.zscaler.com/client-connector.
6. Zscaler. Choosing the CA Certificate for SSL Inspection. help.zscaler.com/zia/choosing-ca-certificate-ssl-inspection. See also: Zscaler. SSL Inspection in Developer Environments. zscaler.com/blogs/product-insights.
7. Zscaler. About Access Policy — ZPA. help.zscaler.com/zpa/about-access-policy.

PART IV

The Governance Lens

Migration governance, risk governance, and political governance—
the disciplines that determine whether
transformation holds under pressure.

Chapter 9

RAID Is Not Optional

Risk discipline in Zero Trust programs

PRE-MORTEM applied to security transformation.
Real-time execution control under pressure—
Risk, Issues, Assumptions, Dependencies as active signals, not static logs.

There is a moment in every program where execution begins to drift.

Not visibly.

Not immediately.

But subtly.

A dependency is assumed instead of confirmed.

A risk is acknowledged—but not owned.

An issue is discussed—but not contained.

An assumption is carried forward—unchallenged.

Nothing breaks.

Not yet.

But control begins to weaken.

This is where most programs fail.

Not because RAID was missing—

but because RAID was treated as documentation

instead of control.

RAID is not a report.

It is the operating system of execution.

What this chapter addresses is not the existence of RAID—

but the gap between RAID as artifact and RAID as control—

the gap where most Zscaler programs lose their grip.

9.1 Risk: The Signal Before Failure

What risk actually represents. Why unmanaged risk becomes inevitable failure.

Risk is not uncertainty.

It is early visibility.

A risk exists because something is not yet proven:

An application dependency

An identity mapping

A certificate trust path

An endpoint behavior

A third-party integration that has never been tested through the new path

Risk does not mean failure—

but unmanaged risk guarantees it.

A risk is something that might impact delivery.

An issue is something that already has.

A program where risks consistently become issues is not managing risk.

It is treating risk as artifact—

without taking action.

Documentation records risk.

Management reduces it.

Real-world execution:

A ZPA rollout includes an application assumed to be fully mapped.

A minor dependency is identified—
an internal service call.

It is logged.

But not owned.

Not validated.

Not scheduled.

During rollout—the application fails.

Not because the system broke.

But because the risk was real—

and untreated.

A risk marked "accepted"
without accountable ownership
is not acceptance.

It is avoidance.

Disciplined acceptance is different.

It names the owner.

It names the impact the program is willing to absorb.

It names the trigger—

the condition under which the accepted risk must be revisited.

Acceptance without those three is not a decision—

but a deferral.

Control requires structure:

A risk must have an owner,
a validation path,
and a defined moment of proof.

If not—

it does not belong in RAID—

it belongs in a parking lot of unfinished thinking—

or better yet—

in documentation pretending to be governance.

Governance does not document risk—
It forces risk to move.

9.2 Issue: The Moment Control Is Tested

What defines an issue. Why response—not occurrence—defines program strength.

Issues are not unexpected.

They are inevitable.

In a Zscaler implementation:
A policy mismatch,
An authentication failure,
A certificate trust conflict,
A mobile enforcement inconsistency,
A forwarding-profile collision with another agent—
These are not anomalies.

They are execution realities.

What matters is not whether issues occur.
What matters is:
How quickly they are identified.
How clearly they are isolated.
How decisively they are resolved—
and whether they lead back to the risk that should have caught them earlier.

Real-world execution:

A wave rollout begins.

Users authenticate successfully—

but cannot reach a specific application.

The issue is raised.

A weak program:

Debates ownership

Delays escalation

Continues rollout

A controlled program:

Isolates scope

Pauses the wave

Engages the correct owners

Resolves before proceeding

Then returns to the risk register to ask: should we have seen this?

Execution reality:

An issue does not define failure.

Delayed response does.

Severity must be defined before ownership.

Not by volume.
Not by urgency.

By impact.

Control requires authority—

the ability to pause the wave
before the problem spreads.

Without it—
execution continues.

But control does not.

9.3 Assumptions: The Hidden Instability

Why assumptions are the most dangerous element of RAID. What happens when assumptions are not validated.

Assumptions are silent.

They do not raise alerts.

They do not generate logs.

They do not escalate themselves.

But they shape execution.

Common assumptions in Zscaler programs:

All applications are fully documented

Identity attributes are accurate

Group memberships reflect current employment status

Endpoints behave consistently within a single OS family

Certificate trust is universal across application stacks

Policy ordering reflects the intended access decision

These assumptions are rarely true.

An assumption allows execution to proceed
without evidence.

Real-world execution:

A policy is designed based on group membership.

The assumption: group data is accurate.

During rollout—access behaves inconsistently.

The issue is not policy.

The issue is identity integrity.

The system did not fail.

It executed exactly as defined.

The assumption was wrong.

Execution reality

Assumptions are not neutral.

They are untested risk.

If an assumption is not scheduled for validation—
it is not controlled.

Scheduling an assumption for validation means three things.

The assumption is named explicitly—

not implied.

A validation method is defined—

what evidence will prove it true or false.

A deadline is set—

the moment by which the assumption must either become fact or become risk.

An assumption without those three—

is not part of the program—

but part of its blind spot.

"Everyone knows"
is not evidence.

It is exposure.

9.4 Dependencies: The Invisible Architecture

What dependencies really represent. Why dependencies fail under pressure.

Dependencies are not always visible.

They exist between:
Applications (north-south and east-west service calls).
Identity providers (federation chains, attribute sources).
Certificate chains (root, intermediate, application-specific stores).
Network paths (DNS, routing, MTU, latency-sensitive workflows).
Endpoint behavior (agent forwarding decisions, OS-level networking stacks).
External parties (SaaS allowlists, partner gateways, regulatory file transfers).

In design—dependencies appear linear.
In execution—they behave dynamically.

A dependency validated in isolation
can still fail under—
load,
timing,
or sequence.

Real-world execution:

An application is fully mapped.
Access is granted through ZPA.

The application loads successfully—
but fails during a background process.

The missing dependency: a secondary service call not captured in discovery.
The system appears functional.
Until it is not.

Execution reality
Dependencies do not fail in isolation.
They fail under load, timing, and sequence.

Dependency governance is therefore not a map—
it is a sequence.

Each dependency must answer four questions:
What does it depend on—upstream
What depends on it—downstream
Under what conditions has it actually been observed—not assumed
What happens when it is unavailable—and who is notified

A dependency that has only been validated under design conditions
has not been validated.
It has been imagined.

Execution will test the difference.

9.5 RAID as a Real-Time Control Model

Why RAID must be active — not static. How Technical Project Managers enforce control.

RAID is often maintained as a document.
Updated weekly.

Reviewed periodically.
Reported upward.

That is not control.

Control requires:
Real-time visibility
Active ownership
Continuous validation
And immediate response

RAID must live inside execution:
Risks tied to validation checkpoints
Issues tied to rollout decisions
Assumptions tied to verification steps
Dependencies tied to deployment sequencing

RAID is not reviewed here—
but operated.

Technical Project Managers do not write RAID—
They operate it.

That distinction is structural.

Writing RAID is administrative.
Operating RAID means driving entries to closure on a defined cadence.
Forcing ownership when ownership drifts.
Escalating stagnation before it becomes failure.
Refusing to accept the words "still in progress" as a status.
"Still in progress" is not a status.
It is the absence of one.

Execution reality

A RAID entry without movement
is not stable.

It is stagnant.

Stagnation creates risk.

Control requires motion.

9.6 The Execution Bridge: Where RAID Becomes Real

Live coordination during rollout. Decision-making under pressure.

Every serious rollout requires a bridge.

Not a meeting.

A control point.

During execution:

Systems generate signals.

Users report experience.

Engineers interpret behavior—

and decisions must be made

in real time.

RAID becomes the structure of that conversation.

Real-world execution:

A rollout wave is in progress.

Risk exists.

Issue emerges.

Assumption is challenged.
Dependency is unclear.

The bridge forces alignment:

Confirm scope.

Isolate impact.

Decide action.

Continue?

Pause?

Rollback?

That decision is not instinct.

It is RAID-driven control.

Execution reality

The bridge is not a discussion forum.

It is a decision system.

If RAID is not updated during the bridge—
control is already behind.

The Technical Project Manager decides.

Someone else records.

Control requires separation of roles.

A bridge dissolves into a meeting when three things happen.

Status replaces decision—

participants describe instead of decide.

Ownership becomes shared—
which means it is owned by no one.

The next action is not assigned before the bridge ends.

When those three appear—
the bridge is no longer a control point.

It is a forum—
And forums do not deploy.

9.7 PRE-MORTEM: Surfacing Risk Before RAID Has Anything to Govern

The upstream discipline that determines what RAID will need to manage.

RAID assumes risk has already been identified.

That is its limitation.

A risk that has not been surfaced cannot be tracked.
An assumption that has not been challenged cannot be validated.
A dependency that has not been named cannot be agreed.

The discipline that solves this gap is not RAID—
It is PRE-MORTEM—
And, it reveals what is not yet visible.

The PRE-MORTEM concept was originally introduced by cognitive psychologist Gary Klein in his 2007 Harvard Business Review article "Performing a Project Premortem" as a structured exercise to imagine project failure in advance and identify its likely causes before work proceeds.

In "Cloud Migration PM Bible™", this concept is extended into the PRE-MORTEM Risk Discovery Framework — a formal, repeatable methodology that integrates failure-first thinking directly into enterprise execution.

The reframing is simple:
Instead of asking "what risks do we think might happen?" —
PRE-MORTEM asks:
"The initiative has failed. What caused it?"

This is not philosophical.
It is operational.

Once failure is assumed:
Hidden dependencies surface
Optimistic planning collapses
Control becomes the objective

In a Zscaler program, PRE-MORTEM exposes:
Undocumented application dependencies
Unscalable segment design
Coexistence assumptions
Undefined decommission triggers
Identity hygiene gaps

PRE-MORTEM is not a workshop.
It is a discovery instrument.

It must be executed:
Before architecture is locked
Before pilot waves
Before each transition
Before decommissioning

Execution reality

RAID manages visible risk.

PRE-MORTEM makes risk visible.

One without the other—

is incomplete control.

9.8 — Control Checkpoint

The conditions under which a Zscaler program can claim it is controlled.

A Zscaler program is not controlled because it is progressing.

Progress is a measurement of motion.

Control is a measurement of intent.

The two are not the same.

A program can move quickly and still be uncontrolled.

A program can move slowly and still be controlled.

Speed proves capability.

Control proves the program can stop,

decide,

and resume—

on purpose.

A program is controlled when risk is actively reduced:

When issues are resolved in time

When assumptions are validated

When dependencies are understood

When RAID is operated—not reviewed

When the bridge drives decisions.

When failure has been simulated.

Only then—

is execution controlled.

Closing Principle

RAID is not a formality.

It is not a report.

It is not a project artifact.

It is the difference between:

execution that survives
and execution that collapses under pressure

Programs do not fail because RAID is missing.

They fail because RAID is ignored—

until it is too late.

And RAID alone is not enough.

RAID governs what is visible.

PRE-MORTEM reveals what is not.

Together—

they convert uncertainty into control.

A principle carried forward from Cloud Migration PM Bible™ —

"Most teams prepare for success.

High-performing teams prepare for failure.

Because when failure is anticipated—
it can be governed.

And when it is governed—
it no longer dictates the outcome.

Control is not documented.
It is enforced."

References

1. Project Management Institute (PMI). (2021). A Guide to the Project Management Body of Knowledge (PMBOK® Guide) (7th ed.). PMI — risk discipline and project outcomes.
2. Axelos. (2023). Managing Successful Projects with PRINCE2® (7th ed.). The Stationery Office — RAID log practices, risk vs. issue distinction, assumption and dependency management.
3. Klein, G. (2007). Performing a Project Premortem. Harvard Business Review, 85(9), 18–19. https://hbr.org/2007/09/performing-a-project-premortem.
4. Noël, G. L. (2026). Cloud Migration PM Bible™ — PRE-MORTEM Risk Discovery Framework™.
5. Zscaler. ZPA Policy Evaluation Behavior (first-match logic). Zscaler Help Portal. https://help.zscaler.com/zpa

Chapter 10

Political Architecture

Why execution fails at the leadership layer

Power, language, and influence in enterprise transformation.
Control is not only technical—
it is organizational in structure and behavior.

There is a point in every transformation—
where the architecture is no longer technical.

It becomes political.

Not because the technology is unclear.
Not because execution is uncontrolled.
But because the organization itself—
is not aligned.

Zscaler implementations do not fail—
because they are technically complex.

They fail—
because they disrupt existing power
structures.

That disruption is not accidental.

It is inherent.

Because Zero Trust does not simply introduce
a new technology.

It changes:
who controls access—
how access is enforced—
where authority resides

And when authority shifts—
resistance follows.
Execution does not fail in the architecture.

It fails—
in the organization.

10.1 The Language Problem

Why truth cannot always be stated directly. How language determines acceptance.

Every project begins with an objective—
a business requirement.

What the business needs to achieve—
and why.

What problem are we solving?

What outcome does the business expect?

In theory,
that objective should be clear,
direct,
and shared.

In practice—
it rarely is.

A Zscaler implementation may have a true objective:
Eliminate legacy VPN
Transition to Zero Trust
Centralize access control

But stating that objective directly—
can destabilize the program.

Real-world execution:

The organization was using Viscosity—
a commercial OpenVPN client developed by SparkLabs—
as its remote access solution.

The strategic direction was clear:
Move away from VPN
Install Zero Trust
Adopt the full Zscaler stack

But one constraint existed:
The stakeholder who owned the VPN platform—
held significant influence—
And did not align with the direction.

Stating the objective as "VPN replacement"
would not create alignment.

It would create resistance.

And resistance at that level—
does not slow a project.

It stops it.

So, the objective had to be reframed.
Not changed.
Reframed.

"Modernizing access architecture"
"Enhancing security posture"

"Improving application-level control"

The intent remained the same.

The language changed.

Reframing is not deception.
Deception conceals the objective.
Reframing chooses the language—
through which the objective is introduced.

The architecture does not change.

The scope does not change.

The outcome does not change.

What changes—
is the order in which the organization is invited
into the truth.

That distinction is the line—
between political skill and political dishonesty.

Cross it—
and trust collapses.

Respect it—
and trust becomes the medium
through which the program moves.

In enterprise environments—
language is not communication.

It is a form of control.

10.2 The Power Structure Reality

Why ownership determines influence. How existing systems create political gravity.

Every system has an owner.
And ownership creates influence.
The more deeply a system is embedded—
across operations, dependencies, and behavior—
the stronger its influence becomes.

VPN is not just a tool.

It is:
operationally critical
widely used
deeply trusted
politically protected

Replacing it is not a technical decision.

It is a political event.

Real-world execution:

The VPN owner was not simply responsible
for a system.

He represented continuity.
Operational stability.
Established trust.

Introducing Zscaler was perceived as
Modernization.
It was perceived as:
Disruption.
Loss of control.
Erosion of ownership.

That perception matters.

Because perception drives behavior.

Behavior is what the program actually encounters.
Not the org chart.
Not the approved plan.
Not the stated direction.

Behavior is the meeting attended late.
The data not shared.
The decision deferred until the next cycle.

Perception produces those behaviors quietly—
quietly,
and consistently.

Technology changes systems.

Perception determines—
whether the change is allowed.

10.3 The TPM in the Middle

Neutral role, non-neutral environment. Balancing execution with organizational dynamics.

The Technical Project Manager is expected
to be neutral.

But the environment is not.

Execution demands:
Clarity
Alignment
Accountability

Politics introduces:
Resistance
Selective communication
Hidden agendas

The TPM operates between both.

Real-world execution:

The project required:
Application inventory
Dependency mapping
Access validation

The VPN owner controlled critical knowledge
needed for discovery.

But alignment was not guaranteed.

The TPM could not force compliance,
expose full intent,
or escalate prematurely.

Those constraints defined the boundary of the role.

And yet—
execution depended on cooperation.

This is where the role changes.

From coordinator—
to strategist.

A TPM does not control people.

They control—
how execution moves through people.

10.4 Structured Communication as a Control Mechanism

What is said—
and what is not said.
Designing communication intentionally.

Not all information should be shared equally.
That is not deception.
It is controlled communication.

In politically sensitive programs:
Messaging must be intentional

Timing must be controlled

Audiences must be considered

Real-world execution:

It requires a communication structure:

What is communicated to leadership

What is communicated to stakeholders

What is communicated to engineering teams

This creates a language framework:

Strategic language for alignment

Operational language for execution

Controlled disclosure for sensitive transitions

The objective is never hidden.

It is sequenced.

Communication is not about transparency alone—

It is about timing, framing, and impact.

Sequencing has limits.

It does not withhold requirements from those who must build to them.

It does not deny scope to those whose work depends on it.

It does not leave decision-makers without the information they need to decide.

Sequencing controls the order of disclosure.

It does not eliminate disclosure.

When sequencing crosses into omission—

it stops being communication strategy.

It becomes risk.

10.5 The Dependency Paradox

When the people resisting the change are required to enable it.

This is one of the most critical realities in enterprise transformation:
The individuals who resist change—
are often the ones required to enable it.

In this case:
The VPN owner—
was essential to:
Application discovery
Access pattern validation
Operational insight

Without that input—
ZPA could not be implemented correctly.

This creates a paradox:
Execution depends on cooperation—
from those who may not support the outcome.

The solution is not confrontation.

It is controlled engagement:
Involve them in discovery
Position their expertise as critical
Align contribution without triggering resistance

Resistance cannot always be removed.

But it can be redirected into contribution.

Redirection is not flattery.

It is recognition—
that resistance often contains expertise
the program cannot replace.

The VPN owner knew:
Which applications relied on the VPN—
in ways no inventory captured.
Which user populations would be
affected first.
Which exceptions existed quietly—
inside the existing model.

That knowledge is not optional input.
It is required input.

Asking for it—
on its own terms—
converts the source of resistance—
into the source of insight.
The outcome does not change.
The path to the outcome—
becomes navigable.

10.6 Stage Gates vs. Political Reality

Why formal governance alone is not enough. Sign-off does not guarantee alignment.

From a project management standpoint:

Stage gates

Approvals

Sign-offs

should create clarity.

In reality—

they often create illusion.

A stakeholder may sign off:

Without full agreement

Without full understanding

Or under organizational pressure

That does not create alignment.

It creates temporary compliance.

Real-world execution:

Formal governance existed.

Approvals were documented.

But resistance remained—

unspoken.

Until execution reached a critical point.

Sign-off does not equal support.

It only confirms acknowledgment—

not alignment.

Alignment is visible in behavior, not signature.

Does the stakeholder volunteer information without being asked?
Do they bring their team into the program rather than gate access to it?
Do they raise risks early—
or only at the moment of failure?

Those signals reveal alignment more reliably than any approval document.

A signed approval with absent behavior—
is a deferred problem.

Not a resolved one.

10.7 Designing Political Architecture

How to operate within organizational reality. Building structure beyond technical execution.

Political architecture must be intentional.
It includes stakeholder mapping.
Using a named framework—
power and interest, salience, or a hybrid of both.

It includes influence analysis.

Who moves whom.

It includes communication strategy.
Tiered, timed, and documented.

It includes dependency alignment.
Who must cooperate, and on what terms.
And it includes escalation pathways.
Defined before they are needed.

This is not separate from execution.

It is execution.

A controlled political architecture ensures resistance is anticipated.

That communication is structured.

That dependencies are navigated.

That decisions are timed correctly.

Without it—

execution becomes reactive.

With it—

execution remains controlled.

10.8 Control Checkpoint

The conditions under which a Zscaler program can claim it is organizationally aligned.

A Zscaler program is not aligned
because the plan is approved.

It is aligned
when organizational dynamics are managed.

The program must demonstrate
that stakeholder influence is understood and mapped.

Using a named framework.

Power and interest—
plotting each stakeholder
against how much influence they hold
and how invested they are in the outcome.

Salience—
ranking stakeholders
by power,
legitimacy,
and urgency.

Or a hybrid
that combines both views.

The program must demonstrate
that communication is structured
and intentional.

With audience
and timing defined.

That resistance is identified—
and actively managed.

Not assumed absent.

That critical dependencies
are aligned with execution.

Not parallel to it.

And that sign-offs
are backed by observed behavior.

Not only signatures.

Only then—
can execution proceed
without hidden disruption.

Closing Principle

Technology does not operate in isolation.

It operates inside organizations.

Organizations have:

Power structures.
Competing interests.
Established ownership.
Resistance to change.

Ignoring that reality—
does not simplify execution.

It guarantees failure.

Execution is not only technical.

It is organizational.

And the Technical Project Manager—
must be able to operate in both.

References

1. Project Management Institute. A Guide to the Project Management Body of Knowledge (PMBOK® Guide) (8th ed.) and The Standard for Project Management. PMI, 2025. Stakeholder Performance Domain; stakeholder definition; engagement principle.
2. Project Management Institute. The Standard for Program Management (5th ed.). PMI, 2024. Program manager's responsibility for navigating stakeholder motivations.
3. SparkLabs Pty Ltd. Viscosity — OpenVPN Client for macOS and Windows. sparklabs.com/viscosity.
4. Bourne, L. and Walker, D.H.T. Stakeholder engagement in projects, cited in Project Management Institute, Engaging Stakeholders for Project Success, PMI Learning Library.
5. Mitchell, R.K., Agle, B.R., and Wood, D.J. "Toward a Theory of Stakeholder Identification and Salience: Defining the Principle of Who and What Really Counts." Academy of Management Review 22(4), 1997, pp. 853–886.
6. Mendelow, A.L. "Environmental Scanning: The Impact of the Stakeholder Concept." Proceedings of the Second International Conference on Information Systems, 1981. Adapted as the Power/Interest Matrix in Johnson, G. and Scholes, K., Exploring Corporate Strategy (5th ed.), Prentice Hall, 1999.
7. Prosci, Inc. Best Practices in Change Management — 12th Edition: Executive Summary. Prosci, 2023. Sponsorship as the #1 contributor to change success since 1998.
8. Kotter, J.P. "Leading Change: Why Transformation Efforts Fail." Harvard Business Review 73(2), 1995, pp. 59–67; and Leading Change, Harvard Business School Press, 1996.
9. PMBOK, PMI, and related marks are registered trademarks of Project Management Institute, Inc. Viscosity and SparkLabs are trademarks of SparkLabs Pty Ltd. OpenVPN is a trademark of OpenVPN Inc.

PART V

The Adoption Lens

Technology delivers capability. Adoption delivers outcome.

Chapter 11

Zero Trust Fails Without Human Trust

Behavior determines whether architecture survives

Adoption is not support—
it is transformation.

Control fails when behavior reverts.

There is a point in every transformation where the system works—
and still fails.

Access is configured.
Policies are enforced.
Traffic is controlled.

And yet—
users find ways around it.

They reconnect to legacy systems.
They request exceptions.
They recreate old access paths.

Not because they are resisting the organization.

Because they are following habit.

This is where Zero Trust fails in practice.

Not in architecture.

Not in execution.

In behavior.

A system does not succeed because it is implemented.

It succeeds when behavior aligns with it—
and is sustained.

The data confirms what execution already shows.

Most transformations fail for one reason—
people do not change with the system.

The architecture is not where programs fail—
Behavior is.

11.1 — The Persistence of Legacy Behavior

Users do not return to the past out of resistance. They return because it feels familiar.

Users do not change because systems change.

They change when their behavior changes.

In a Zscaler transformation, VPN is replaced with application-level access.

Broad connectivity is replaced with restricted reach.

Implicit trust is replaced with enforced verification.

From a technical standpoint—
this is correct.

From a human standpoint—
it is disruptive.

Legacy systems feel:
Familiar
Predictable
Trusted

Even when they are less secure.

Real-world execution:

The new system is in place.

ZPA is functioning.

Policies are enforced.

And still—users request VPN access.
They rely on old workflows—
avoid the new system when possible.

Not because the system failed.

Because behavior did not change.

Users do not resist change.

They revert to familiarity under pressure.

A workaround is not sabotage.

It is a signal.

It tells you the system does not align with behavior—yet.

11.2 — The Illusion of "Go-Live"

Go-Live is not success. It is exposure.

There is a dangerous moment in every project:

Go-Live.

It signals completion.

But in reality—
it signals the beginning of truth.

Because once a system is live:
Users interact
Workflows are tested
Behavior is revealed

Real-world execution:

Leadership declares success.
The system is operational.

But support tickets rise.
Exceptions increase.
Users request workarounds.

This is not failure.

This is reality surfacing.

Go-Live is not the finish line.

It is the starting point of adoption.

That distinction changes the program's posture.

Before Go-Live, the work is building.

After Go-Live, the work is observing.

Before Go-Live, success means the system is ready.

After Go-Live, success means the user is.

The team that delivered the implementation
is not the team that delivers the adoption.

And the program
that does not recognize that shift
treats Go-Live as the end—
when it is the beginning.

11.3 — ADKAR as Execution Discipline

Adoption must be structured—not assumed. From awareness to reinforcement.

Adoption is not organic.

It must be engineered.

Most programs believe communication equals adoption.

It does not.

Users may understand the change—
and still not follow it.

The ADKAR model, developed by Prosci founder Jeff Hiatt in the 1990s, frames adoption as a sequence of five conditions an individual must move through for change to take hold.

Awareness—why this is happening.
Desire—why it matters to me.

Knowledge—how it works.
Ability—can I actually use it.
Reinforcement—will I continue using it.

The model is sequential.

Each stage must be reached before the next becomes possible.

Most programs stop at knowledge.
They explain.
They train.
They document.

But they do not verify whether the user can operate in the new model.

Whether the user will stay in the new model.

Knowledge is the cheapest stage.

It is the one a program can complete with a slide deck and a calendar invite.

Ability requires practice.
Reinforcement requires time.

Both cost more than a program plan typically reserves for them.

Which is why both are the first to be cut—
and the first to cause adoption to collapse.

Awareness explains change.
Reinforcement sustains it.

If any stage is missing—
adoption breaks.

And when adoption breaks—
control collapses silently.

11.4 — Preparing Users Before the Change

Why timing determines success. Behavior must shift before enforcement. Control enforced without preparation creates resistance by design.

Users must be prepared before enforcement.

Not during.

Not after.

Before.

Preparation means:

Clear communication
Clear impact
Clear expectations
Clear demonstration

Clear communication is not a single announcement.

It is a sequence.

What is changing.
When it is changing.
And what the user must do differently when it does.

Clear impact means the user knows which workflows will behave differently—
named explicitly.

Not described in general terms.

Clear expectations mean the user knows what is required of them—
and what is not.

Clear demonstration means the user has seen the new model work
before they are asked to depend on it.

Preparation without those four—
is not preparation.

It is notification.

Real-world execution:

Zscaler is deployed.

Users are informed at the same time.

The result:

Confusion.
Frustration.
Resistance.

Because behavior
was expected to change—
without preparation.

Change is not accepted because it is correct.

It is accepted because it is understood.

11.5 — The Role of Influential Stakeholders

Why leadership alignment is not enough. Influence must cascade through the organization. Behavior does not follow policy.

It follows influence.

Not all stakeholders carry the same weight.

Some define direction.

Others define behavior.

Managers.
Senior engineers.
Operational leads—
If they do not align—
their teams will not follow.

Real-world execution:

Leadership supports the change.

But a key operational leader—

questions the change.

Delays adoption.

And signals hesitation.

That signal spreads.

The team follows the signal—

not the architecture.

Alignment at the top is not enough.

Alignment must cascade.

Alignment at the top is not enough.

Alignment must cascade.

From leadership—
to management.

From management—
to execution teams.

From execution teams—
to the users expected to operate within the change.

Otherwise—
alignment becomes localized.

And execution fractures beneath it.

Behavior does not follow policy—
It follows influence in practice.

11.6 — Breaking Legacy Habits

Why reinforcement is required. What happens when old systems remain accessible.

As long as legacy systems remain available—
users will return to them.

This is not resistance.

It is habit.

This creates a critical decision point:
If the new system is introduced—
but the old system remains unrestricted—
adoption will stall.

Real-world execution:

If VPN remains available—
users will choose:

What they know
What is easier
What requires less change

The result:
Dual behavior
Inconsistent control
Incomplete transition

A new system cannot succeed—
if the old system remains easier.

Coexistence is temporary.

Or it becomes permanent.

Coexistence is a transition state—
not a destination.

And the Technical Project Manager
is the one
who must defend
the decommissioning trigger—
against the organizational gravity
that will always prefer
the familiar path.

11.7 — Reinforcement as a Control Mechanism

Ensuring behavior does not revert. Making the new model the default.

Reinforcement is not optional.
It is structural.

Without reinforcement—
users revert.

Reinforcement means:
Removing legacy paths
Enforcing new access patterns
Monitoring behavior
Correcting deviation

This is not punishment.

It is control.

Reinforcement is where adoption becomes permanent.

Reinforcement does not end at deployment.

It runs in parallel with operations.

It measures whether the new model is being used—
not whether it is available.

Availability is a system property.

Use is a behavior.
A program
that measures only availability
will declare success—
while adoption
silently erodes.

Reinforcement requires
three disciplines
to continue working:

Visibility—
the program must see
how users are actually behaving.

Response—
deviation must be corrected—
not absorbed.

And recognition—
the users who operate
within the new model
must be acknowledged
so, the new model becomes
the path of least friction—

not the path of greatest effort.

11.8 — Control Checkpoint

The conditions under which a Zero Trust implementation can claim transformation—not deployment.

A Zero Trust implementation is not successful because it is deployed.

It is successful:

When users operate within the new model
When legacy usage declines
When stakeholders reinforce behavior

Deviation is corrected—
and adoption is measured—
not assumed.

Decommissioning trigger is defended, not deferred.

Only then—
has transformation occurred.

Closing Principle

Organizations that ignore behavior deploy successfully—
but fail operationally.

Organizations that manage adoption align behavior.

Reinforce change.
Sustain control.

Zero Trust does not fail because of architecture.

It fails when people do not trust—
or adopt—
the change.

Control does not fail because it is weak.

It fails because it is not sustained.

And that is where the Technical Project Manager completes the work.

Technology defines control.

Behavior determines whether control holds.

References

1. Boston Consulting Group — Digital Transformation Success Study — Organizational factors drive success more than technology
2. McKinsey & Company — Digital Transformation Survey — People-centric factors dominate outcomes
3. Gartner — Zero Trust Implementation Survey (2024) — Adoption gaps drive failure rates
4. NIST — Security Fatigue Research — Behavioral response to repeated security demands
5. Prosci — Change Management Benchmarking — Adoption and reinforcement determine success
6. Hiatt, J. M. (2006). ADKAR: A Model for Change in Business, Government and Our Community. Prosci Learning Center Publications — Five-stage individual change model (Awareness, Desire, Knowledge, Ability, Reinforcement)
7. PMI — PMBOK Guide (7th Edition) — Recognition of structured change frameworks
8. Kotter — Leading Change — Influence and coalition-driven adoption
9. Zscaler ThreatLabz — VPN Risk Report — Behavioral persistence of legacy access

PART VI

The Execution Lens

Where command, sequencing, and reversibility are tested under live conditions.

Chapter 12

The Execution Command Center

The Technical Project Manager's Control Room

Where Zscaler enforcement is directed—
not assumed. Where coordination determines whether Zero Trust holds.

Execution does not fail in planning.

It fails in coordination.

When a Zscaler program reaches live deployment,

structure alone is no longer enough.

Policies are defined.

Application segments are configured.

Identity is integrated.

Zscaler Client Connector is deployed.

And still—

execution can collapse.

Not because the architecture was wrong.

Not because Zscaler was insufficient.

But because control was never established in real time.

This is where the Execution Command Center becomes necessary.

It is not a meeting.

It is not a status forum.

It is not a place to observe execution.

It is where execution is directed—

while the system is live,

while traffic is flowing,

while decisions carry immediate consequence.

This chapter is organized in two parts.

Part A describes the command center during cutover—the war room, where decisions are measured in minutes.

Part B describes what comes after—the steady-state operational command that runs the platform long after the cutover team has gone home.

Both are the same discipline.

They operate at different speeds.

The war room ends.

The platform does not.

PART A — Live Cutover Command

12.1 — What an Execution Command Center Actually Is

Real-time control of Zero Trust enforcement. Not a status meeting.

An Execution Command Center is a centralized control structure where Zscaler enforcement decisions are made, validated, and adjusted across all control planes.

It exists for one purpose.

To ensure that Zscaler behaves as designed—
when reality begins to diverge from expectation.

In theory, Zscaler enforces policy precisely.

In practice, enforcement depends on identity state:
On endpoint posture
On traffic steering behavior

On application definition accuracy

Execution does not break loudly

It drifts—
until it fails.

The Command Center exists to manage that reality.

It is where ZPA access behavior is validated.
Where ZIA traffic enforcement is observed.
Where ZCC endpoint behavior is confirmed.
Where policy decisions are adjusted in real time.

Without it, enforcement becomes inconsistent.

And inconsistent enforcement—
under pressure—
becomes perceived failure.

This is not a new discipline.

It is the same command model
used in incident response
and production—
applied to a Zero Trust rollout
while the traffic is live.

Running is not success.

Enforcement is.

Instinct is not control.

Execution is.

12.2 — Roles: Ownership Meets Execution

Clarity of roles is the first condition of control.

Zscaler does not live in one domain.

It lives across all of them.

Security defines policy.
Identity determines access.
Endpoint enforces behavior.
Network influences traffic.
Applications define what access actually means.

Each domain can be correct on its own.

And still fail together.

Zscaler does not fail within a domain.

It fails at the intersection of them.

The Command Center forces alignment across:

Security— policy definition, risk posture, Zero Trust enforcement.
Identity— IdP behavior, group membership, authentication integrity.
Endpoint— Zscaler Client Connector deployment, posture, certificate state.
Network— DNS resolution, traffic steering, routing behavior.
Application owners— application definitions, FQDN accuracy, dependency validation.

Vendor support— platform insight, edge behavior, escalation support.
PMO — execution coordination across all domains.

Each domain controls a piece of Zscaler.

But no domain controls Zscaler alone.

That responsibility belongs to coordinated execution.

Not for discussion—
For decision.

Because execution does not fail inside silos.

It fails in the gaps between them.

12.3 — War Room Structure During Cutover

Every change is live. Every participant is accountable for a signal.

During Zscaler cutover, the Command Center becomes a war room.

This is where:
VPN coexistence is being reduced
ZPA is taking over application access
ZIA is enforcing internet traffic
ZCC is actively steering behavior
Everything is live

Every participant is accountable for a signal:
"User cannot access application"
"Traffic not routing through ZIA"

"Authentication succeeded—but access denied"
"ZCC installed—but not enforcing policy"

A signal is not a problem—
It is a request for interpretation.

This is where teams fail.

They assign the issue too early.

In Zscaler:
What appears as a network issue is often policy
What appears as policy is often identity
What appears as identity is often endpoint

Misinterpretation is not delay—
It is misdirection.

The war room is not about visibility.

It is about decision discipline—
and controlled.

Cutover is where theory ends.

12.4 — Decision Flow Under Pressure

When something breaks, execution accelerates.

Not slows down.

And that is where mistakes happen.

Real-world execution:

A user reports:

"I cannot access the application."

That is not a problem.

It is a signal.

Interpretation must consider:

Whether the application segment defined correctly.
Whether the user is in the correct IdP group.
Whether ZCC is enforcing traffic through ZPA.
Whether DNS is resolving through the Zscaler path.

Validation requires cross-domain confirmation—
not assumption.

The ZPA Admin Portal Diagnostics,
ZDX deep trace,
ZCC logs,
and NSS streams
each reveal
a different perspective
of the same transaction.

No single tool tells the whole story.

Control is confirmed only when signals align.

What this means in execution is simple—
but rarely implemented.

Signals do not move in sequence.

They emerge simultaneously—
across identity, endpoint, network, and policy.

Without structure—
they fragment.

The Command Center exists to force convergence.

The structure below is not conceptual.

It is the control model—
that governs execution when the system is live—
where signal converges to one point, and decision originates from authority.

The diagram below shows how that convergence is structured in live execution—
six signal domains, one decision authority, two possible outcomes.

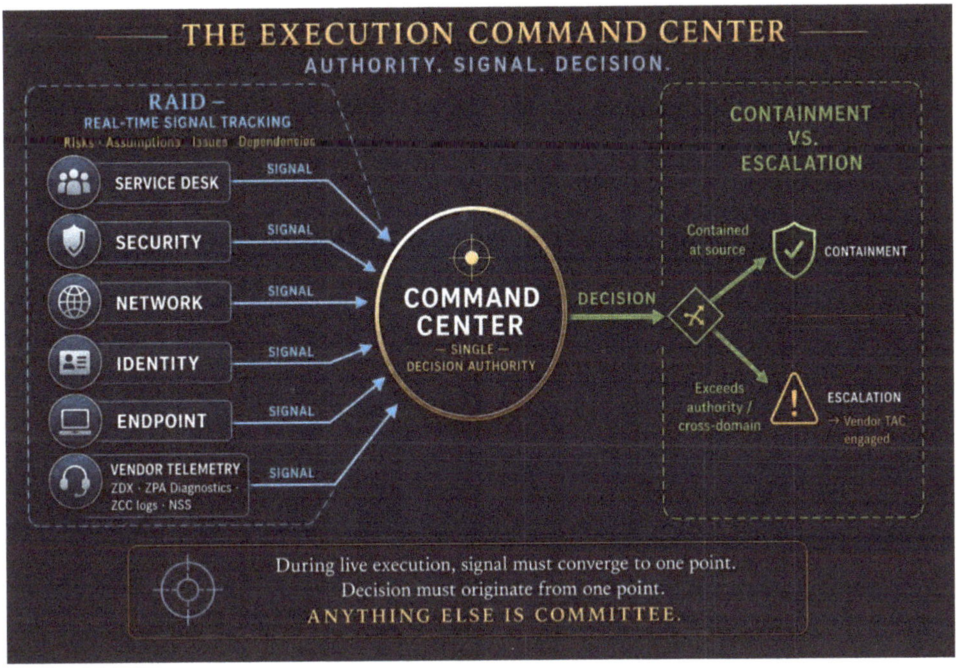

Six signals.

One authority.

One decision.

Containment or escalation—

never both,

never by committee.

That is the control model.

Everything in this chapter operates inside it.

This is the difference between coordination and control.

In real execution,

every domain

produces a valid signal—

and all of them can be correct.

And still, execution fails.

Because correctness is isolated.

Control is convergence.

From this point forward—
execution is no longer about identifying signals.

It is about controlling:
Who speaks
How signals are validated
And where decisions are made

Execution follows one path:

Signal → Interpretation → Validation → Action

Skip interpretation—you guess.
Skip validation—you assume.
Act too early—you move the problem.

A moved problem is more dangerous than an open one.

Because it looks like progress.

In Zscaler, every layer must be verified:
Application segment definition
Identity-to-policy group mapping
ZCC enforcement state at the endpoint
DNS resolution and traffic steering behavior
Failure emerges at the intersection.

Control is not speed.

Control is accuracy under pressure.

In Zscaler, problems rarely exist where they first appear.

What looks like a network issue, an access failure, or an application outage
is often a policy misalignment, an identity condition, or an endpoint enforcement gap.

Control is not restored by reacting.

It is restored by understanding
how enforcement behaves across layers—
in real time.

Accuracy under pressure is—
what the war room exists to produce.

12.5 — Communication Under Pressure

Communication is not open during execution.

It is controlled.

Every team sees a different truth:

Security sees policy
Network sees traffic
Identity sees authentication
Endpoint sees device behavior

Multiple truths exist.

Only one must drive action.

Without control:

Voices overlap
Decisions delay
Actions conflict

Execution does not fail from silence.

It fails from noise.

Clarity is not helpful under pressure.

Clarity is control.

Because pressure changes
how organizations behave.

Under stress,
people do not naturally move toward order.

They move toward reaction.

Teams begin interpreting signals differently.
Multiple voices attempt to direct execution.
Assumptions replace validation.
Escalations accelerate faster than understanding.

And noise—
begins competing with reality.

That is why mature execution models
reduce communication paths
instead of expanding them.

One voice drives decisions.
One channel validates truth.
One channel communicates outward.

Because under pressure—
clarity is not merely communication.

It is containment.

It is stabilization.

It is operational control.

12.6 — Real-Time Signal Tracking (RAID in Execution)

Zscaler is continuously evaluating. Problems do not wait.

RAID is not documentation.

It is live awareness.

Zscaler does not wait.

Access fails immediately.
Policy misaligns instantly.
Identity drifts continuously.
Endpoint behavior changes unpredictably.

Problems do not queue.

They propagate.

In live execution, those signals appear as:

Application access failures—visible in ZPA diagnostics and access logs.
Policy mismatches—in ZIA policy evaluation and audit logs.
ZCC enforcement gaps—client state, forwarding behavior, posture drift.
Identity misalignment—SAML assertion failures, SCIM synchronization drift.
Certificate and trust failures—SSL inspection breakage, pinned application behavior.

These are not tracked after execution.

They are tracked during enforcement.

Because Zscaler is not static.

It is continuously evaluating.

And that means:

Problems do not wait.

The RAID log a program review on Monday—
is not the RAID log that determines outcome on Wednesday.

Wednesday's log is the one being maintained in real time—
in the minutes between signals.

The weekly risk register is a lagging artifact.

The live RAID board is a leading one.

The Command Center tracks:

What is breaking
What is at risk

What is changing
What is unresolved

Visibility does not solve problems.

It makes control possible.

12.7 — Failure Containment vs Escalation

Zscaler failure is rarely total. It is usually localized misalignment.

Containment isolates the problem.

Escalation expands the response.

Not all issues require escalation.

But during cutover—

every issue feels urgent.

Most Zscaler failures are not platform failures.

They are misalignment:

Identity mismatch
Application misdefinition
Endpoint inconsistency

This is where execution judgment matters.

A field guide:

A single application misconfiguration is contained
An identity-wide access failure is escalated
A ZCC deployment inconsistency is contained
A platform-level enforcement anomaly is escalated to Zscaler TAC

The execution decision is not based on visibility alone.

It is based on blast radius.

Escalate everything—
and you lose control.

Contain everything—
and you miss real failure.

Choose incorrectly—
and you do not delay execution.

You destabilize it.

12.7.1 — The Containment Test

Before you escalate, ask three questions.

In order.

Scope.

Is the failure bounded?

One app. One user. One segment.

Or is it crossing identity, policy, trust boundaries, or platform enforcement behavior?

Bounded—contain.

Crossing—escalate.

Reproducibility.

Can you reproduce it on demand?

Reproducible and bounded—
contain.
Fix in place.

Reproducible and unbounded—
escalate.

Intermittent—
instrument first.

Never escalate a ghost.

Origin.

Configuration or enforcement?

Yours or the platform's?

Configuration failures are contained.

Enforcement failures are escalated.

That line is the line between you and TAC.

Because the real question is no longer:
"Can the issue be fixed?"
The question becomes:
"Can trust still be assumed?"

That is the real escalation threshold.

12.7.2 — The Default Posture

If you cannot answer the three questions in five minutes—contain.

Escalation without diagnosis is noise.

And noise during cutover is indistinguishable from failure.

The platform team begins responding to your panic.

Not your problem.

12.7.3 — The Override

Identity-wide access failure overrides the test.

Escalate immediately.

Diagnose in parallel.

Blast radius compounds by the minute.

12.8 — Control Checkpoint

At any point in execution, one question matters:

Is Zero Trust still enforcing correctly?

That means:

Correct users
Accessing correct applications
Under correct conditions
Through correct enforcement paths

If not—

Zscaler is still running.

But control is not.

And in Zero Trust—
Running is not success.

Enforcement is.

PART B — Steady-State Operational Command

The war room ends.

The platform does not.

The Hypercare Bridge

Between Command Center control and steady-state operation—there is a gate.

Hypercare is not a phase.

It is a decision point.

It is where execution proves
that control can survive
without the war room.

During cutover,
control is directed.

During operation,
control must sustain itself.

Hypercare is the bridge between the two.

In a Zscaler program, this is where:

Command-center intensity begins to step down
Service desk assumes routine signal handling
Operations absorb runbooks, dashboards, and thresholds

The program team remains present—but no longer leads.

This transition is not time-based.

It is condition-based.

Thirty, sixty, ninety days—
these are conventions.

They do not determine readiness.

Control does.

The program does not exit hypercare
because time has passed.

It exits when control is demonstrably stable.

That means:

Runbooks are validated under real conditions.
Identity, policy, and endpoint enforcement behave consistently.
Incident volume stabilizes within defined thresholds.
Operations can interpret and act without escalation dependency.
SLAs and SLOs are accepted as operational reality—not projection.

Hypercare is not observation.

It is reinforcement.

It is where:
Assumptions are removed
Behavior is corrected
Control is sustained

Exit it too early—
and execution regresses silently.

Remain too long—
and ownership never transfers.

This is not a balance of time.

It is a balance of control.

Control Gate—

The question is no longer:

"Is the system running?"

The question becomes:

"Will control hold—without us?"

Only when that answer is yes—
does the Command Center release execution
to the operating model.

The war room hands over to the platform team.

What it hands over determines what survives.

12.9 — From Command Center to Operating Model

Execution pressure becomes operational discipline.

What was once controlled in minutes—
must now be sustained for years.

Drift is not failure.

Unchecked drift becomes failure.

The team changes.
The discipline does not.

The steady-state operating model for a Zscaler platform has a defined structure:

Platform ownership becomes singular
Execution becomes distributed
Control becomes continuous

Platform ownership becomes singular—
held by a Product Owner accountable for the Zscaler platform.

Security Operations sustains threat monitoring, policy tuning, and SIEM correlation.
Network Operations maintains DNS, routing, bandwidth, and tunnel health.

Identity Operations governs IdP health, group lifecycle, and SCIM provisioning. Endpoint Operations manages the ZCC lifecycle, posture enforcement, and update profiles.

Application Owners continuously validate application segment definition.

The Change Advisory Board governs change under ITIL-aligned enablement.

Zscaler TAC and Professional Services define the escalation boundary and platform health cadence.

Each function owns a domain.

No function owns control alone.

What the Command Center enforced in real time—
the operating model must now sustain without coordination overhead.

The Incident Commander does not disappear.

The role becomes distributed—
absorbed into on-call rotations and operational response.

The Communications Lead becomes the service desk
and stakeholder rhythm.

The Operations Lead becomes platform engineering.

The structure changes.

The responsibility does not.

Control is no longer maintained by presence.

It is maintained by discipline.

The organism is the same.

The metabolism is different.

12.10 — Change in a Live Zscaler Platform

Every change introduces risk.

Too slow—irrelevance.
Too fast—instability.

Control is not stopping change.

It is enabling safe change.

In a Zscaler environment, change does not occur in isolation.

A policy update affects access.
An identity change affects enforcement.
An endpoint shift affects behavior.

Blocking change does not create stability.

It freezes the current state—
while risk continues to evolve around it.

Control requires structured change.

Not avoidance.

Three change types govern execution:

Standard—
low-risk, pre-authorized, repeatable.

A new application segment aligned to an approved pattern.

Normal—
risk-assessed, authorized, domain-aware

A ZIA policy change impacting a user population.
Emergency—
time-critical, security-driven, post-validated.

A rapid enforcement change during an active incident.

Each type carries a different level of control.

Standard change scales execution.
Normal change protects coordination.
Emergency change preserves control under threat.

Authority must match proximity.

The closer the team is to the change—
the faster and more accurate the decision.

Centralized approval creates delay.

Uncontrolled delegation creates risk.

Control exists in the boundary between the two.

Change success is not defined by approval.

It is defined by outcome.

A platform that approves everything—
has no control.

A platform that fails every fourth change
—is not enabling change.

12.11 — Reliability Is Measured, Not Assumed

Users experience reliability—not architecture.

Reliability is not uptime alone.

It is consistent access.

Predictable behavior.

Enforced control.

If access degrades—
the platform is failing.

Even if everything appears operational.

Perception does not define reliability.

Behavior does.

Reliability must therefore be measured against the user—
not against the platform.

Uptime measures whether the service is reachable.

Reliability measures whether the user can do their work.

Those are not the same metric.

A Zscaler platform can be ninety-nine-point nine percent available

and still be unreliable—
if access is slow during peak hours,
if authentication prompts cascade unexpectedly,
if certain applications behave differently for certain populations.

Reliability discipline requires three things to be defined.

What good looks like—
in terms the user would recognize.

What degradation looks like—
before it becomes outage.
And what the program will do when reliability drops —
before the user has to ask.

12.12 — Learning from Failure

Failure is not the problem.

Failure without learning is.

Every issue reveals something:

A missed dependency
An incorrect assumption
A gap in coordination

If ignored—
it repeats.

Learning from failure is not a retrospective.

It is a discipline.

A retrospective produces a document.

A discipline produces a change.

And the change must be visible—
in the runbook,
in the policy,
in the detection rule,
in the validation step that would have caught it earlier.

A failure that produces a document but not a change
has not been learned from.

It has been recorded.

And what is recorded without correction

will recur—
usually under worse conditions than the first time.

12.13 — Policy Decay Problem

Rules accumulate.

Rule-sets do not self-clean.

Policies accumulate.

They do not self-correct.

Exceptions grow.
Rules expand.
Access broadens.

Growth is not control.

Uncontrolled growth is exposure.

Zscaler inherits this reality:
ZIA URL categories expand
ZPA application segments multiply
SCIM-governed groups evolve
Posture profiles change
Exception paths accumulate

Not all growth is intentional.

Some of it is:
Orphaned rules
Shadow rules
Redundant rules

The platform does not become cleaner over time.

It becomes heavier.

And what grows without discipline—
becomes risk.

Steady-state control requires deliberate reduction:

Quarterly access review—
across users, groups, application segments, exceptions, policy-hit behavior.

Unused policy pruning—
because rules that do not execute are not dormant.

They are candidates for removal

Exception lifecycle enforcement—
because every exception must expire.

Otherwise, it becomes policy in disguise

Policy-as-code where possible—
version-controlled,
peer-reviewed,
auditable.

Growth alone creates risk.

Control requires subtraction.

12.14 — Continuous Improvement Loop

Zscaler is not deployed once.

It is refined continuously.

Telemetry is not observation.

It is input for decision.

If metrics do not drive action—
they are noise.

Zero Trust is not a completed state.

It is a continuously enforced condition.

Static policy slows the system.

Unvalidated change destabilizes it.

Control exists in the loop between the two.

A Zscaler platform operates as a feedback system:

Signals are generated
Signals are interpreted
Decisions are made
Decisions are validated

And then—
the cycle repeats.

The signals that matter are not abstract.

They are operational:

Access denials
Policy mismatches
Traffic anomalies
Identity drift
Endpoint enforcement gaps
User experience degradation

These are not metrics to observe.

They are signals to act on.

Analysis gives direction.

Decision creates change.

Validation confirms control.

If validation fails—
the change is reverted.

Not defended.

Because in Zscaler—
persistence is not
proof of correctness.

Validation is.

A dashboard that is watched but not acted on—
is not visibility.

It is delay.

Collection alone is not Zero Trust.

Action is.

Zscaler does not improve over time—
unless decisions are continuously made against real signals.

And that loop—
must never stop.

If telemetry does not change behavior—
control is already decaying.

12.15 — Final Control Checkpoint

Deployment is a moment.

Operation is a discipline.

If control is not sustained—
the platform exists.
But Zero Trust does not survive.

A Zscaler platform is not running because it is deployed.

It is running because it is governed.

In steady-state operation, control is visible:

Change success is measured
Reliability is defined and tracked
Incidents produce learning—not repetition
Policy decay is identified—and reversed
Telemetry drives decisions—not reports
Ownership is clear—and authority is real

If these conditions do not exist—
the platform is present.

But control is not.

And without control—
execution does not degrade.

It disappears.

Deployment is a moment.

Operation is a discipline.

Execution determines survivability.

Closing Principle

Control is not maintained by configuration.

It is maintained by command.

The Technical Project Manager who stands up the war room
and hands off the platform
has not finished the work.

They have only completed the first half.

The second half is steady state—
quieter,
longer,
more patient.

Zero Trust is not a project that ends.

It is a platform that must be commanded—
continuously, for as long as the enterprise exists.

And command—

must be continuous,
intentional,
and enforced under pressure.

Enforcement determines reality.

References

1. National Institute of Standards and Technology (NIST). Computer Security Incident Handling Guide (SP 800-61).
   — Basis for structured incident response and command-style coordination.
2. Beyer, Betsy, et al. Site Reliability Engineering: How Google Runs Production Systems. O'Reilly Media.
   — Foundations for real-time incident management and operational control.
3. Project Management Institute (PMI). The Standard for Program Management.
   — Governance, coordination, and cross-domain execution principles.
4. Zscaler, Inc. Zscaler Support & Architecture Documentation.
   — Platform behavior, ZIA/ZPA/ZCC enforcement, and operational considerations.
5. Cybersecurity and Infrastructure Security Agency (CISA). Zero Trust Maturity Model.
   — Framework for continuous Zero Trust evolution and operational maturity.

Chapter 13

The Wave Model

Risk-based, non-linear execution

The wave model is not chosen.

It is imposed by the system's constraints—
because without it, control does not survive execution.

Execution does not move in a straight line.

It moves in waves.

Not because organizations prefer it—
but because the system cannot be operated any other way.

In Zscaler installations, this becomes unavoidable.

You are not migrating systems.

You are redefining how access behaves:
Across users
Across applications
Across endpoints
Across identity providers
Across policy engines
Across the invisible paths that once defined trust

Each element evolves at a different pace.
Each carries its own risk.
Each exposes its own failure.

Execution cannot remain continuous under these conditions.

It must be segmented.

That segmentation—
is the wave model.

A wave is not a batch.

It is not a schedule.

It is not a deployment group.

A wave is a controlled exposure of the system to reality.

And if that exposure is not deliberately constructed—
it does not fail quietly.
It fails operationally.

Zscaler enforces what it is told—
immediately.

There is no grace period.

No interpretation.

No forgiveness for what was not defined.

That is the discipline a wave imposes.

13.1 — Why Waves Fail in Real Organizations

Waves do not fail because of timing.

They fail because of assumptions.

The most common failure pattern is structural.

A wave is defined by population—
not by control readiness.

Users are grouped.

Devices are selected.

A rollout date is assigned.

Execution begins.

But the architecture underneath is incomplete.

Applications are partially defined.
Dependencies remain hidden.
Identity attributes are inconsistent.
Endpoint posture varies.

Policy behavior is assumed—

not proven.

The wave appears successful—
until real usage begins.

Simulation 13.1 — The Friday Cutover

A regional bank executes Wave 1.
2,400 users. Friday evening.

ZCC is deployed.
PAC file is pushed.

ZPA segments are configured for primary applications.

Saturday produces no incidents.
The program declares success.

Monday, 08:14—first failure.

Users access the application.
Authentication succeeds.
Sessions establish.

Then transactions fail.

The backend dependency was never defined as a segment.
Under VPN, the backend was reachable—
because the VPN granted a routable corporate IP.

Under ZPA, the backend does not exist.

Not because it is unreachable—
because it was not declared.

ZPA does not infer.
It does not extend access to what looks adjacent.
It enforces exactly what was configured—

and nothing else.

By 09:30, multiple applications fail in the same pattern.
Front-end defined.
Back-end invisible.

The architecture did not break.

It executed—exactly as configured.
By 11:00, a temporary wildcard segment restores access.

By Wednesday, segmentation is corrected.

The lesson is not failure.

The lesson is precision:

Population readiness was mistaken for application readiness.

The users were ready.
The system was not fully defined.

And the cause remains consistent:

The wave was executed before control was proven.

A wave is not a deployment event.
It is a validation boundary.

If that boundary is weak—
everything beyond it becomes unstable.

13.2 — The Myth of Linear Progression

Organizations expect progression to behave predictably:

Wave 1 → success
Wave 2 → improvement
Wave 3 → scale

That expectation does not hold.

Each wave introduces a different operating condition:
New applications
New dependencies
New behaviors
New failure paths

Wave 2 is not an extension of Wave 1.
It is a different system state.

Complexity does not reduce.
It compounds.

Simulation 13.2 — The Wildcard That Broke Stability

Wave 1 stabilizes cleanly.
Defined FQDNs. Controlled ports. Predictable behavior.

Wave 2 introduces a wildcard segment:

*.corp.internal

Discovery begins.

So does amplification.

App Connector CPU increases sharply.
Health-check cycles slow from seconds to minutes.
Wave 1 applications begin degrading.

Nothing is malfunctioning.

Everything is overloaded.

The wildcard instructs every connector to resolve every matching FQDN.

To multiply each resolved address across every open port.

And to probe all of them on every cycle.

The system is not behaving unpredictably.

It is doing exactly what it was instructed to do.

The correction is surgical:

Scope the wildcard.
Limit the ports.
Isolate connector groups.

Stability returns.

The lesson is structural:

A wildcard is not a discovery mechanism—

It is a load multiplier with a discovery side-effect.

Execution does not scale linearly.

It escalates.

13.3 — Wave Collision

Where execution loses clarity — when a new wave begins before the previous one has stabilized.

Wave collision is where execution loses clarity.

It occurs when a new wave begins
before the previous one has stabilized.

Two conditions exist simultaneously:

Unresolved issues from the prior wave—

and new variables introduced by the next.

Traceability collapses.

Simulation 13.3 — The Untraceable Loop

Wave 1 remains active.
Wave 2 begins under schedule pressure.

New users are onboarded.
A second identity federation is introduced.

Then a failure appears.

Users enter authentication loops.

No component is visibly broken.

The IdP responds correctly.
ZPA enforces policy correctly.
ZCC behaves as designed.

But an attribute—
modified during Wave 2—
is no longer present on a subset of Wave 1 users.

A Wave 1 access policy still requires that attribute.

ZPA evaluates the policy.
The attribute is missing—
access is denied.

ZPA does not flag the change.

It does not warn that an upstream condition has shifted.

It enforces the policy as written—
against the data it now receives.

ZCC interprets the denial as an authentication failure.

The user re-authenticates.
The session returns.
The attribute is still missing—the loop continues.

Six hours to isolate.

Not due to technical complexity—
but due to lack of clarity across waves.

Every component was honoring its instruction.

The failure lived in the gap between two waves' instructions—
which the architecture had no obligation to reconcile.

Wave collision does not accelerate execution—
It destroys visibility.

Without visibility—
control cannot be maintained.

And when control is lost—
the system continues operating
without explanation.

That is not execution.

That is unmanaged exposure.

13.4 — Risk-Based Wave Sequencing

Waves are not ordered by convenience.

They are ordered by survivability.
Convenience prioritizes scale.

Survivability prioritizes control.

Execution must begin where failure can be absorbed.

Foundation first.

Then controlled exposure.
Then increasing complexity.
Then edge conditions.

Not because it is slower—
but because it is the only sequence that holds.

Simulation 13.4 — Two Programs, One Outcome Difference

Division A begins with scale.
Mission-critical systems.
High-risk dependencies.

Source-IP allowlisted partner feeds.

Non-interactive service accounts with no posture context.

Division B begins with control.
Low-risk users.

Clean FQDN-defined applications.

Single data center.

No partner dependencies.

Six weeks later:

Division A is overwhelmed.

Service accounts are denied access—

because the policy requires posture,

and the accounts cannot provide it.

The architecture is not failing.

It is enforcing—

precisely—

the conditions

the program had not yet earned

the right to enforce.

Rollback begins.

Division B progresses.
Control is proven.
Next wave advances.

Same platform.

Same configuration model.

Different result.

Only one difference:

Sequencing.

This is not optimization.

It is survival.

Because high-risk failure does not degrade.

It escalates.

The sequence is not a preference. It is a structure.

The model below shows how the waves
behave across time—

where they accelerate,
where they must pause,
where they collide,
and where they feed back into discovery.

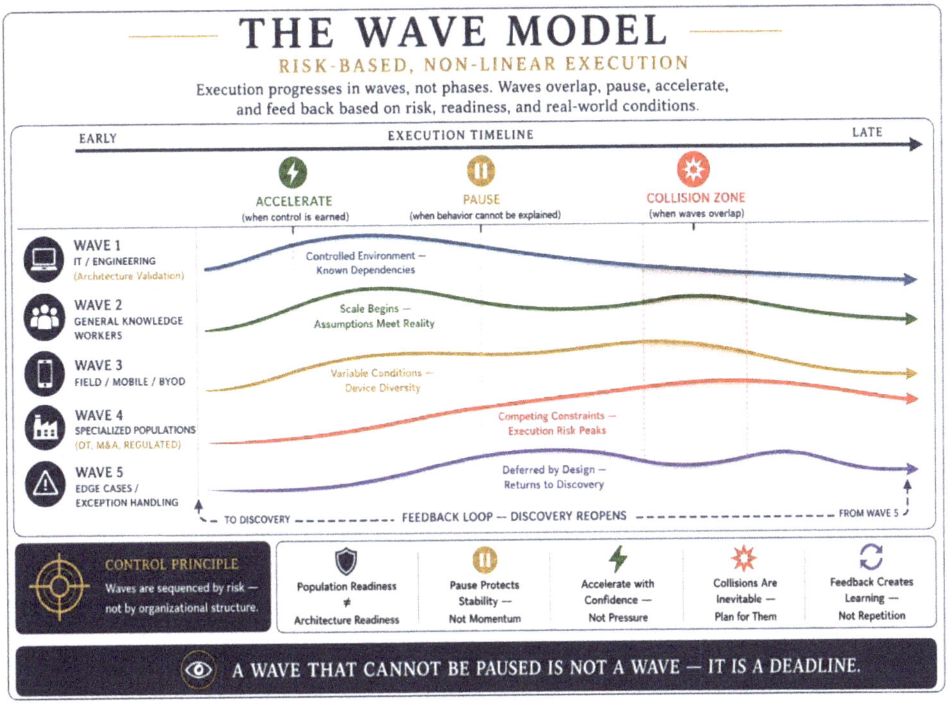

Figure 13.1 The Wave Model — Risk-Based, Non-Linear Execution.

The waves are visible.

The control points are not automatic.

Each one—
pause,
acceleration,
collision,
and feedback—
must be enforced as a discipline.

What the diagram names—
the next four sections enforce.

13.5 — When to Pause a Wave

Pausing a wave is not failure.

It is the enforcement of control.

A wave must pause when behavior cannot be explained.

Not approximated.

Not assumed.

Explained.

Simulation 13.5 — The Pause That Preserved Control

A healthcare organization progresses through Wave 2.

An inconsistency appears.

Same application.

Same policy.

Different outcomes across endpoints.

The issue is initially dismissed as environmental.

The program pauses.

Nine days later—root cause:

A posture profile evaluates a registry condition.

On newer agent builds, the evaluation runs in one security context.

On older builds,
it runs in another—
and on a subset of endpoints,
that context cannot read the value.

The check fails silently.

ZPA receives a non-compliant posture.

Access is denied.

The agent does not warn that the evaluation context changed.
The policy does not flag that posture results are now divergent.
The architecture enforces the result it was given—
immediately, and without interpretation.

1,800 endpoints would have been migrated—
into a state where access—
to the clinical application could not succeed—
in active clinical environments.

The pause cost time.

The alternative would have compromised operations.

Momentum without explanation is not progress—

It is exposure that has not yet been measured.

13.6 — When to Accelerate

Acceleration is not driven by schedule.

It is driven by proof:
Consistency
Predictability
Stability
Clarity

When these are present—
execution can move faster.

When they are absent—
speed becomes illusion.

Simulation 13.6 — Earned vs. Forced Acceleration

One program stabilizes Wave 2.
Metrics improve.
Tickets decline.

Support resolves independently.

They advance—
and Wave 3 inherits a stable foundation.

The architecture continues enforcing the same conditions,
predictably,
because nothing about the underlying definitions has changed.

Another advances under pressure:
Instability remains
Metrics degrade
Execution continues

Wave 3 inherits Wave 2's unresolved definitions— and adds new ones on top.

The architecture does not slow down to accommodate the gap.

It enforces every instruction it now holds—
both the unstable ones and the new ones—
with the same immediacy.

Failure follows.

Rollback begins.

Both moved forward.

Only one progressed.

Acceleration must be earned.

Not declared.

Earned means four conditions can be demonstrated—
not asserted.

Consistency—
the same instruction produces the same result across the population.

Predictability—
the failure modes are known, and recur in expected places.

Stability—
the system holds under load, not only under design conditions.

Clarity—
every signal can be traced to a defined cause.

When those four are present—
acceleration is a measured decision.

When any one is absent—
acceleration is a gamble.

And the architecture does not distinguish between the two.

It enforces both with the same precision.

13.7 — Wave Feedback Loops

Every wave must inform the next.

If it does not—
failure repeats.

Each wave reveals:
Dependencies that were not mapped
Policy gaps that were not visible
Identity inconsistencies that were not aligned
Endpoint variations that were not accounted for
Brokering patterns that were not expected

If these signals are not captured—
they compound.

Simulation 13.7 — The System That Learned

A disciplined program executes across waves.

After each wave—
signals are captured and converted.

Dependencies discovered through wildcard segments
become defined segments.

Wildcards are retired before the next wave inherits them.

Policies are tightened before later waves load more sensitive applications.

Identity attributes are reconciled at the source.

Endpoints are standardized.

Connector group topology is adjusted.

Each wave removes failure from the next.

By the final wave—
the most complex conditions operate cleanly.

Not by chance—
by design.

This is not optimization—

It is survival.

Because Zero Trust is not static.

It evolves—
with every execution cycle.

Closing Principle

Waves do not exist to move faster.

They exist to control exposure.

Organizations that fail:

Push volume.
Measure activity.
Assume progress.

Organizations that succeed:

Sequence by risk.
Validate behavior before scale.
Advance only when control is proven.

In Zscaler execution—
a wave is not a milestone.

It is a confrontation with reality.

And reality does not adapt to the plan.

The plan must adapt—
to reality.

References

1. Zscaler, Inc. Zero Trust User-to-App Segmentation with ZPA — Reference Architecture.
   — Foundational model for application segmentation, policy enforcement, and ZPA architecture behavior.
2. Zscaler, Inc. ZPA Leading Practices Guide.
   — Operational guidance for segmentation design, App Connector behavior, and scalable deployment patterns.
3. Zscaler, Inc. Zscaler Client Connector Deployment & Troubleshooting Guides.
   — Endpoint enforcement, posture verification, authentication flows, and failure mode diagnostics.
4. Zscaler, Inc. ZIA SSL Inspection Leading Practices Guide.
   — SSL inspection phasing, certificate trust distribution, and controlled rollout strategy.
5. National Institute of Standards and Technology (NIST). Zero Trust Architecture — Implementation Guidance (SP 800-207 / NCCoE Builds).
   — Policy engine design, identity dependency, and Zero Trust enforcement principles.

Chapter 14

Rollback Is a Leadership Discipline

Risk appetite, exercised under pressure

Rollback is the only mechanism by which leadership exercises authority—
over a system that cannot exercise judgment over itself.

It is not failure.

It is control—
reasserting itself.

Rollback is not a backup plan.

It is a requirement.

Every complex migration,
cloud transformation,
systems upgrade,
or application modernization—
must have a way back.

Without it—
execution stops being controlled.
And becomes exposure.

Zscaler does not fail quietly.

When control breaks, it manifests immediately:

Users lose access

Applications behave unpredictably

Authentication loops occur

Traffic paths fragment

The architecture has no opinion about whether to continue.

It will keep enforcing—
whatever it was last told.

In those moments—
the decision is not technical.

It is leadership.

"Continue forward—
or restore control."

That decision is not made by the platform.

It is not made by the engineers.
It is not made by the dashboards.

It is made by a leader—
operating within the boundaries
of what the organization is willing to absorb.

Rollback is where leadership and risk appetite meet the architecture.

14.1 — Why Organizations Resist Rollback

Organizations resist rollback for one reason: momentum.

Time has been invested.
Resources have been committed.
Stakeholders expect progress.

And rollback feels like:
Delay
Failure
Loss of confidence

But that perception is false.

In Zscaler execution,
The danger is rarely rollback itself.

The danger is continuing forward
without restored control.

When teams continue forward:
unresolved policy inconsistencies persist
endpoint behavior remains unstable
identity conditions are not aligned
application access is partially functional

The system does not stabilize.
It fragments.

That tells why organizations resist—
risk appetite was never defined.

When leadership has not stated—
how much disruption the business is willing to absorb—
every rollback decision becomes a debate.

And debates do not happen at the speed Zscaler enforces.

Rollback is resisted—
because it is misunderstood.

It is not retreat.

It is control refusing to proceed
without proof.

14.2 — The Cost of Forced Forward Motion

Forward motion without control creates compounding failure.

In Zscaler environments, this is immediate:

Wave 1 produces issues.
Wave 2 introduces new variables.
Wave 3 amplifies both.

Failures begin to overlap:

Is it ZPA segmentation?
Is it ZCC enforcement?
Is it identity drift?
Is it certificate trust?

The system becomes untraceable.

Support teams escalate everything.
The Execution Command Center loses signal clarity.
Decision-making slows.

And the organization reaches a point where:
no one can explain what is happening—

only that it is getting worse.

Meanwhile, the architecture, is doing exactly what it was told.
As it has no mechanism to slow itself down.

It does not pause to let the operator catch up.

This is not execution.

This is collapse under momentum.

Rollback prevents that collapse.

14.3 — Rollback Decision Triggers

Rollback must not be emotional.

It must be triggered.

In Zscaler execution, rollback conditions are clear:
Access behavior is inconsistent across identical users
Applications partially function or intermittently fail
Policy outcomes differ by device or path
Identity-based access produces unpredictable results
Endpoint posture signals are unreliable
Traffic cannot be clearly traced through ZIA or ZPA paths

The most critical trigger
is when you cannot explain the failure.

If execution cannot explain behavior—
control does not exist.

And if control does not exist—
execution must stop.

Rollback is not optional at that point.

It is required.

But triggers alone do not produce action.

A trigger only matters if a leader is authorized to pull it—
and that authority must be granted before the wave begins.

Not negotiated during the failure.

In disciplined programs:
Rollback authority is pre-assigned.
Threshold is documented.
Decision-maker is named.

When the trigger is met—
the leader acts.

No meeting.
No escalation chain.
No approval cycle.

Because Zscaler does not wait for governance.

Pre-assigned authority requires three things to exist before the wave begins:

A named decision-maker—
with the authority to halt execution without requiring further approval.

A documented trigger threshold—
expressed in terms the Command Center can observe in real time.

And a pre-validated rollback sequence—
the named decision-maker is empowered to invoke.

Without those three—
the trigger fires
and no one is empowered to act on it.

And in Zscaler execution—
delay is enforcement.

The architecture continues.

The exposure compounds.

14.4 — Controlled Reversion vs. Panic Reversal

Not all rollback is equal.

There are two forms:

Panic reversal:

Unplanned
Reactive
Uncoordinated
Executed under pressure

This creates:

New instability
Incomplete restoration
Additional confusion

And often—

a worse state than before.

Controlled reversion:

Predefined
Tested
Coordinated
Executed through the Command Center

In Zscaler, controlled rollback means:

Reverting traffic steering (ZCC, PAC, GRE/IPSec).
Restoring previous access paths (VPN or legacy proxy).
Disabling new policy enforcement safely.
Preserving identity and endpoint integrity.
Maintaining visibility during the transition.

Rollback must be designed—

before execution begins.

If rollback is improvised—

it is not control.

It is reaction.

Simulation 14.4 — Two Reversions, Two Outcomes

Two enterprises hit the same failure condition during a Wave 2 cutover.

In both cases, ZPA segments are misaligned.

Authentication is looping.
Critical applications are partially reachable.

Enterprise A — Panic reversal:

The decision is made in the moment.

ZCC is uninstalled from a portion of the user population by remote command.

PAC files are removed from browsers manually.

Some users revert to VPN.
Others lose all connectivity—
because the VPN client was decommissioned
three weeks earlier and no one updated the rollback plan.

The Command Center is not in the loop.

Identity sessions are still active in ZPA.

Policies are still enforcing on a subset of devices that did not receive the uninstall.

The result is not a return to a previous state.

It is a third state—
one that did not exist before the wave began,
and one no one designed.

Recovery takes 36 hours.

Enterprise B — Controlled reversion:

The rollback plan was written before Wave 2 launched.

Traffic forwarding rules in ZCC have a documented previous-state profile. The PAC file has a versioned predecessor stored centrally.

The legacy VPN cluster was kept warm for 30 days post-cutover.

ZPA access policies for Wave 2 are tagged and can be disabled as a group, not individually.

The trigger is met.

The named leader authorizes rollback.

The Command Center executes the documented sequence.

Within 45 minutes: ZCC reverts to the previous traffic forwarding profile.

The legacy PAC file is re-pushed.

ZPA Wave 2 policies are disabled in a single action.

Users return to the pre-wave access path.

The architecture is now back in a state it has been in before.

A state that is known.

A state that can be re-entered from cleanly.

Both enterprises rolled back.

Only one of them returned to control.

The difference was not technical skill.

It was that one of them had decided—
before the failure—
what going back actually meant.

14.5 — Leadership Behavior Under Pressure

Rollback is where leadership becomes visible.

Under pressure, leaders reveal themselves:
Some push forward—

to protect timelines.

Some hesitate—
to avoid accountability.

But effective leaders do one thing:
They choose control over optics.

They understand progress without control—
is not progress.

In Zscaler execution, this means:
Pausing a wave.
Restoring stability.
Protecting the environment—

Even when it is unpopular.

This is where organizational risk appetite stops being a document—
and becomes a behavior.

A risk appetite statement that has not been tested under pressure—
is just language.

A leader who invokes rollback—
is the moment that statement becomes real.

If the organization claims low tolerance for service disruption—
and the leader continues forward through a clinical or financial outage—
the appetite was never real.

If the organization claims aggressive transformation posture—
and the leader rolls back at the first ticket—
the appetite was never real.

The leader's decision under pressure
remains the only honest measure of risk appetite
an organization will ever produce.

Because leadership is not measured by speed.

It is measured by control under pressure.

Risk appetite that holds under pressure
requires three commitments made before execution begins.

A defined disruption boundary—
how much business impact the organization will accept before rollback is triggered.

A named leader empowered to enforce that boundary—
without requiring consensus when the pressure arrives.

And an honest acknowledgment of what cannot be absorbed—

named explicitly,

by system,

by population,

by time of day.

Without those three, risk appetite is a paragraph.

With them, it is a control.

14.6 — Communication During Rollback

Rollback without communication creates panic.

In a Zscaler environment:

Users lose access

Applications behave differently

Support tickets surge

Without clear messaging, the organization assumes failure.

Communication must be immediate and structured:

What is happening
Why it is happening
What is being restored
What users should expect

The message must be clear.

This is controlled—

Because perception matters.

If rollback appears chaotic—

confidence is lost.

If rollback appears controlled—
trust is preserved.

There are three audiences—
each requires a different message.

Users need clarity
of what is being restored,
when access returns,
and what to do in the meantime.

Operations and support need orchestration:

Rollback sequence
Validation checkpoints
Escalation path while the reversion

Leadership and the business need framing:
This is a controlled action
The trigger that produced it
The conditions required to re-enter execution

If any one of these audiences hears the wrong version—
the rollback succeeds technically and fails politically.

And political failure ends programs faster than technical failure.

14.7 — Re-Entry Strategy After Rollback

Rollback is not the end of execution.

It is the reset.

The most critical mistake organizations make is
re-entering execution—
without change.

After rollback:
The system must evolve.
Application segmentation must be refined.
FQDN, wildcard, and IP definitions must be
Corrected.
Identity mappings must be validated.
Endpoint posture must be standardized.
And policy logic must be simplified.

The next wave must not repeat the previous one.

Re-entry must be:
Smaller
Controlled
And validated

Because the purpose of rollback is not to go back.

It is to return—
with clarity.

Simulation 14.7 — The Re-Entry That Worked

A logistics company rolls back a Wave 2 cutover after authentication loops affect a major distribution hub.

The temptation is immediate:
Resume in two weeks.
Same scope.
Same population—
with fixes applied.

Leadership refuses.

Re-entry is restructured.

The wave is reduced from 4,000 users to 600.
The segmented applications are cut from 38 to 12.

The wildcard segment that contributed to the original failure is replaced with defined FQDNs.

The posture profile that produced inconsistent results is rebuilt and tested across every supported endpoint build.

The Command Center adds a daily 30-minute checkpoint for the first two weeks.

Re-entry begins six weeks later—
not two.

The smaller wave succeeds.

The next wave inherits a refined architecture—
and adds back the populations and applications that were deferred.

By the time the program reaches the original Wave 2 scope,
it is operating on a system that has been tested,
corrected,
and re-entered with discipline.

The rollback did not delay the program.

The rollback is what made the program possible to complete.

14.8 — Control Checkpoint

Rollback exists for one reason—
to protect control.

Before execution resumes, the system must prove:
Consistent access behavior
Predictable policy enforcement
Stable user experience
Traceable traffic paths
And aligned identity conditions

If those conditions are not met—
execution does not proceed.

Not partially.

Not gradually.

Not at all.

Real-world execution Signal — Zscaler Rollback

A wave is executed.

Within 72 hours, users begin reporting:

Applications load partially.

Authentication loops occur.

Access varies by device.

The Command Center investigates:

ZPA segments are defined.
ZCC is deployed. Identity is functional.
Each component is, in isolation, healthy.

But behavior is inconsistent across the user population.

Root cause emerges over two days:

Wildcard domains expanded access into segments that overlap with another connector group.

Backend dependencies for three applications were never mapped.

The Zscaler root certificate is missing on a subset of contractor endpoints, causing SSL inspection to fail for those users only.

The system appeared operational.

It was not controlled.

The named rollback authority is convened.

The trigger is met:

Behavior cannot be explained
at the user level.

The decision is made—
rollback is the outcome.

The Command Center executes the documented sequence.

Traffic forwarding is reverted at the ZCC profile level.
Wave 2 ZPA access policies are disabled as a tagged group.

The legacy PAC file is re-pushed. The legacy VPN absorbs the displaced sessions.

Stability returns within the hour.

Execution pauses.

Discovery resumes:

The wildcard segment is decomposed into defined FQDNs.

The backend dependencies are mapped and added to the segment list.

The certificate gap on contractor endpoints is
closed through MDM remediation.

The next wave is redefined—not by timeline,
but by control readiness.

And the leader who authorized the rollback did not lose credibility.
The leader gained it.

Because the program is still alive.

Closing Principle

Rollback is not the opposite of progress.

It is the condition that makes progress possible.

Organizations that resist rollback move forward.

Lose control.

And collapse under complexity.

Organizations that embrace rollback pause.
Stabilize.
And regain clarity.

In Zscaler execution—
rollback is not a fallback.

It is a requirement.

Because without a way back—
there is no controlled way forward.

And the way back is not a technical artifact.

It is a leader,
exercising authority that the architecture itself does not possess,
within boundaries the organization agreed to before execution began.

That is the discipline of rollback.

References

The technical assertions in this chapter — traffic forwarding reversion (ZCC, PAC, GRE/IPSec), controlled rollback mechanics, and risk-based decision authority — are aligned with Zscaler's reference architecture and enterprise risk governance frameworks. Key sources include:

1. Zscaler. Traffic Forwarding in Zscaler Internet Access — Reference Architecture. https://www.zscaler.com/resources/reference-architectures/traffic-forwarding-in-zscaler-internet-access.pdf
2. Zscaler. Choosing Traffic Forwarding Methods. Zscaler Help Portal. https://help.zscaler.com/zia/choosing-traffic-forwarding-methods
3. Zscaler. About Forwarding Policies and Control Rules. Zscaler Help Portal. https://help.zscaler.com/zia/about-forwarding-policies
4. NIST. NISTIR 8286A — Cybersecurity Risk and Enterprise Risk Management. https://nvlpubs.nist.gov/nistpubs/ir/2021/NIST.IR.8286A.pdf

PART VII

The Enterprise Reality

Modernization without abstraction. Why the core endures — and how to design with it, not around it.

Chapter 15

Hybrid Is Not Failure

Hybrid is not a temporary condition.

It is not a transitional inconvenience—

And it is not a failure to modernize.

What Hybrid Means in This Context

Hybrid, in this context, does not refer to delivery methodology.

It is not Agile.

It is not Waterfall.

And it is not a blend of execution frameworks.

Hybrid refers to architectural reality.

The coexistence of access models and control layers:

Zscaler—ZIA, ZPA, ZCC.

VPN—network-layer access.

Traditional infrastructure dependencies

This is not optional.

It is the condition under which enterprise systems actually operate.

Execution does not replace one model with another.

It manages both—
simultaneously.

That is why hybrid is not a phase.

It is a state.

It is the natural state of real enterprise systems.

Organizations do not move from legacy to modern in a single motion.

They operate in both—
simultaneously.

That is not weakness.

That is reality.

The assumption that Zero Trust replaces everything
is not just incorrect—
it is dangerous.

Because what is removed is not always understood.

And what is not understood—
reappears in execution.

Hybrid is not what remains when transformation is incomplete—
It is what exists when transformation is real.

15.1 Why Hybrid Exists (Not a Weakness)

Hybrid exists because systems are not isolated.

They are layered.

Interdependent.

Bound to workflows that extend beyond architecture diagrams.

Some systems cannot move.

Some dependencies cannot be rewritten.

Some behaviors cannot be eliminated—
without breaking operations.

These are not theoretical.

A mainframe finance system that authenticates by source IP.
A clinical imaging modality that expects a routable network path to its DICOM server.
A manufacturing OT segment that cannot tolerate inspection latency.
A regulatory file transfer that must originate from a known address.
A vendor appliance that was certified against a network topology that no longer exists.

Each of these is real.

Each of these resists Zero Trust enforcement —
not because the architecture is wrong,
but because the system was designed under a different one.

Zero Trust does not erase those conditions.

It exposes them.

And once exposed—
they must be managed.

Not removed blindly.

Because removal without control is not modernization.

It is disruption.

15.2 Zscaler + VPN Coexistence Models

Zscaler does not eliminate VPN immediately.

It redefines what VPN should be used for.

This distinction must be controlled.
Not assumed.

In practice, coexistence follows patterns:

Model 1 — Parallel Access Model

ZPA governs application-level access.

VPN remains for:

Layer 3 / Layer 4 dependencies
Legacy protocols
Diagnostic functions (ICMP, routing validation)

Control is split.

But intentionally.

Model 2 — Conditional Access Model

ZPA is primary.

VPN is invoked only when:

Application segmentation is incomplete
Dependencies are still being discovered
Edge cases require network-layer behavior

VPN becomes exception-based.

Model 3 — Residual Dependency Model

Zscaler fully governs modern applications.

VPN persists only for:

Legacy systems.
Hard-coded IP dependencies.
Systems not designed to be expressed
as defined application destinations.

In this model—

VPN is no longer access.

It is accommodation.

Each model is valid.

Failure occurs when coexistence is not defined.

Because undefined coexistence creates inconsistent enforcement.

And inconsistent enforcement—

is not control.

The three models are not stages.

They are coexistence patterns —
each valid when defined, each dangerous when assumed.

The model below shows how access is structured under each pattern,
and where the line between control and failure is drawn.

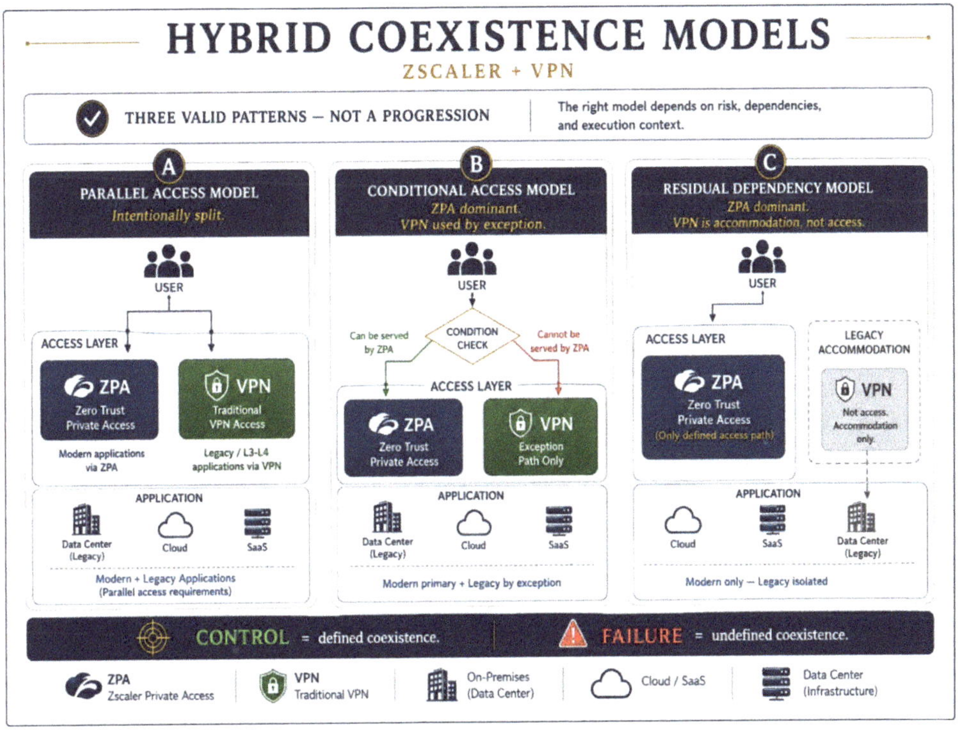

Coexistence can be designed.
Defined coexistence is control.
Undefined coexistence is failure.

And what cannot be designed away—
must be acknowledged.

15.3 Legacy Systems That Cannot Be Eliminated

Some systems cannot be modernized.

Not because organizations lack capability—
but because those systems were never designed to evolve.

They depend on:

IP-based communication
Static trust assumptions
Network-layer reachability
Hard-coded integrations

ZPA does not operate at that layer.

And neither do most modern access platforms.

They enforce access at the application level.

They assume applications can be reached
through identity-aware, brokered access.

Legacy systems were not built for that assumption.

And forcing them into it—
does not modernize them.

It breaks them.

This is not a Zscaler problem.
It is an enterprise reality.

NIST SP 800-207 makes this explicit:

Legacy systems often lack the identity integration,
The APIs, and the authentication models required

to participate in Zero Trust enforcement.

And the implication is direct—
you cannot force Zero Trust onto systems that were never designed for it.

Ryan Galluzzo, Digital Identity Program Lead at NIST's Applied Cybersecurity Division, has stated this directly.

"You can't simply say, we're just going to make everything zero trust.
It's not a realistic goal."

The failure is not technical alone.

It is organizational.

Legacy is not ignored because it is invisible.

It is ignored because acknowledging it slows execution—
and challenges the assumption of a clean transformation.

The system is known.

The dependency is known.

But it is excluded—
because the plan cannot absorb it.

That is the real failure.

Not architecture.

Not tooling.

Avoidance.

These systems must be identified—
not assumed.

Discovery must reflect real traffic, not documentation.

Isolated—
not left exposed.

Containment defines boundaries.

contained—
not forgotten.

Governance must persist beyond configuration.

Not forced into a model they cannot support.

Because execution does not fail when legacy exists.

It fails when legacy is ignored.

And what is ignored in design—
does not remain hidden.

It surfaces—
under load,
under dependency,
and ultimately under pressure.

15.4 Risk of Over-Modernization

There is a point
where modernization becomes risk.

When organizations attempt to eliminate VPN too early,
force all access through ZPA,
remove network-layer capability without replacement.

Hence—

they do not reduce risk.

They create it.

Because dependencies do not disappear.

They become failure points.

Over-modernization introduces:
Broken workflows
Inaccessible systems
Hidden operational gaps

And those gaps do not appear during design.

They appear—

under pressure.

Over-modernization usually does not announce itself.

It looks like progress.

VPN is decommissioned on a schedule—

not on a readiness signal.

Network-layer capability is retired—
before every dependency that relied on it has been mapped.

ZPA is declared the only access path—
while service accounts,
partner integrations,
and legacy diagnostics still depend on something else.

The program looks clean on the slide.

The architecture looks clean in the diagram.

And then a batch job fails at three in the morning,
and the team discovers that the system feeding it lost its access path
when the last VPN node was turned off.

That is over-modernization.

Not a design philosophy.

A schedule that outpaced discovery.

15.5 Hybrid as a Stability Strategy

Hybrid, when designed correctly—
is not compromise.

It is control.

Because it allows:

Gradual transition
Controlled exposure of dependencies
Validation under real conditions

Hybrid provides something pure architectures cannot:

Time.

Time to discover.
Time to validate.
Time to stabilize.

Without destabilizing operations.

That is not inefficiency.

That is disciplined execution.

15.6 Designing Long-Term Hybrid States

Some hybrid conditions do not disappear.

They become permanent.

And that must be accepted—
early.

Designing hybrid requires:

Clear boundaries
Explicit ownership
Controlled access paths
Consistent enforcement

The organization must define:

What remains on VPN
What transitions to ZPA
What requires redesign

Not just once—
But continuously.

Because hybrid evolves.

As dependencies are resolved—
or exposed.

Continuous, in this context, is not constant change.

It is a defined cadence.

A quarterly review of what is still on VPN—
and why.

A standing inventory of exception-based access paths—
with each exception carrying an expiration.

A documented owner for every system that cannot be modernized—
so, accommodation does not become orphan.

And a feedback loop from execution back into design—
so, what was learned in operation
revises the model that produced it.

Without that cadence—
hybrid does not evolve.

It accumulates.

And accumulated hybrid is not architecture.

It is technical debt that nobody scheduled.

15.7 Execution Friction — When Methodology Fails the Architecture

Zscaler is not a linear implementation.

It is aberrational.

It depends on:

Discovery that evolves
Dependencies that surface late
Policies that adapt in real time

Forcing rigid Waterfall execution onto this model—

creates friction.

Because Waterfall assumes:
Requirements are known
Dependencies are fixed
Progression is linear

Zscaler does not behave that way.

It behaves like execution:

Iterative
Conditional
Adaptive

Organizations that force structure without adapting to reality—
do not fail because of Zscaler.

They fail because of rigidity.

Hybrid is not only architectural.

It is operational.

Execution must adapt
to the system being implemented.

15.8 Control Checkpoint

Hybrid is not the absence of control.

It is the test of it.

If coexistence is defined—
control holds.

If coexistence is assumed—
control fragments.

Zscaler does not eliminate legacy.
It exposes it.

And what is exposed—
must be governed.

Because what is not governed—
will not disappear.

It will fail—

when execution begins.

References

1. National Institute of Standards and Technology, Zero Trust Architecture, NIST Special Publication 800-207 (2020). https://nvlpubs.nist.gov/nistpubs/specialpublications/NIST.SP.800-207.pdf
2. Ryan Galluzzo, Digital Identity Program Lead, NIST Applied Cybersecurity Division, quoted in MeriTalk, "NIST Official Urges Unified Zero Trust Approach," February 2026.
3. Cortex, "12 Common AWS Migration Challenges and How to Avoid Them" (2025); Brainhub, "Data Migration: Challenges & Risks During Legacy System Modernization." Both document hidden dependencies — hard-coded IPs, undocumented integrations, batch jobs — as a primary cause of cloud migration failure.

Chapter 16

The Core Never Disappears

The core does not disappear.

It does not dissolve under modernization.
It does not vanish in the cloud.
And it is not removed by Zero Trust.

It changes form.

It changes location.

But it remains.

Organizations believe transformation replaces the core.

That is the illusion.

Transformation does not remove the core.

It obscures it.

And what is obscured—

is no longer understood.

That is where failure begins.

16.1 What "Core" Actually Means

The core is not a system.

It is not a platform.

And it is not a single layer of technology.

The core is the set of conditions required for a system to function:
Identity resolution
Infrastructure availability
Dependency reachability
Control enforcement

Identity resolution—
the system can determine who is requesting access,
and that determination is consistent across every entry point.

Infrastructure availability—
the underlying network, DNS, and routing fabric is present and functional,
because enforcement cannot operate on what cannot be reached.

Dependency reachability—
the services, data sources, and back-end systems an application requires
are accessible through the access model in force.

Control enforcement—
the policy decisions actually apply at the point of access,
consistently, and under real conditions.

Each of these is a precondition.

Not a feature.

Remove any one of these—
and the system does not degrade.

It stops.

That is the core.

It is not what is visible.

It is what is required.

And because it is required—

it cannot disappear.

It can only move.

16.2 Identity as the Permanent Control Layer

In modern architectures, identity becomes the dominant control layer.

Not because infrastructure disappears.

But because control must anchor somewhere.

Identity provides that anchor.

It answers:

Who is requesting access.
What they are allowed to reach.
Under what conditions access is permitted.

Zscaler enforces through identity.

Zero Trust depends on it—

a point established formally by Rose, Borchert, Mitchell, and Connelly in NIST Special Publication 800-207, Zero Trust Architecture, published in 2020 by the National Institute of Standards and Technology.

But identity is not self-sufficient.

If identity resolves—
but infrastructure fails
or dependencies are unreachable
access still fails.

Identity governs access.

It does not guarantee execution.

That distinction matters.

Because many organizations over-rotate—
believing identity replaces the need to understand the underlying system.

It does not.

It shifts the control surface.

16.3 Infrastructure Dependencies That Persist

Infrastructure does not disappear in modern architecture.

It becomes less visible.

Traffic still routes.
Systems still depend on DNS.
Applications still rely on back-end services.
Endpoints still require enforcement mechanisms.

Zscaler operates above these layers.

It does not remove them.

It depends on them.

If DNS fails—
policy cannot resolve.

If routing breaks—
traffic cannot reach enforcement nodes.

If endpoints are misaligned—
control cannot be applied.

These are not edge cases.

They are the foundation.

And when they are not understood—
they are rediscovered under pressure.

16.4 Why Zero Trust Does Not Eliminate Core Systems

Zero Trust redefines control.

It does not eliminate systems.

It removes implicit trust.

It introduces continuous evaluation.

But it does not remove:

Infrastructure dependencies
Protocol constraints
Application behaviors
Operational requirements

Infrastructure dependencies remain—
because the network, the DNS resolvers, the certificate trust stores,
and the enforcement nodes themselves are still infrastructure,
and they still have to be operated.

Protocol constraints remain—
because the applications speak the protocols they were written to speak,
and Zero Trust does not rewrite them.

Application behaviors remain—
because how an application authenticates,
how it sustains a session,
how it tolerates latency,
how it handles inspection,
is determined by the application,
not by the access model in front of it.

Operational requirements remain—
because someone still has to run the platform,
respond to incidents,
and govern change under load.

Zero Trust does not absorb that work.

It redirects it.

Those remain.

What changes—
is how access to them is governed.

Organizations that misunderstand this—
attempt to force Zero Trust as a replacement layer.

It is not.

It is an enforcement model.

And enforcement models require something to enforce.

That something —
is the core.

16.5 Cloud Does Not Remove Complexity

Cloud changes location.

It does not remove complexity.

It abstracts infrastructure.

But abstraction is not elimination.

Dependencies still exist.

They are simply harder to see.

Systems still fail.

But the failure surface is distributed:
Latency replaces locality
Policy replaces perimeter
Visibility requires instrumentation

In a Zscaler context, this is not theoretical.

A SaaS application that worked yesterday
can change its IP range overnight—
and an allowlist that was correct on Monday
is incorrect by Wednesday.

A cloud-hosted application can shift its identity provider integration
without notifying the access tier in front of it.

A traffic path that performs cleanly from one region
can introduce latency from another—
not because the platform failed,
but because the cloud region changed underneath.

None of this is visible in the architecture diagram.

All of it is visible in the user experience.

And when complexity is hidden—
it is often mistaken as removed.

That assumption is dangerous.

Because hidden complexity is harder to control.

Not easier.

16.6 The Illusion of Full Abstraction

The promise of modern architecture is simple:

Everything becomes abstracted.

No infrastructure.
No dependency awareness.
No operational burden.

That promise is incomplete.

Abstraction removes visibility.

It does not remove responsibility.

Someone still owns:
Routing
Identity
Policy enforcement
System availability

And when those responsibilities are not defined—
they do not disappear.

They fragment.

Fragmentation is the final stage of misunderstood control.

Because when ownership is unclear—
execution becomes inconsistent.

And inconsistent execution—

is failure.

16.7 Control Checkpoint

The core never disappears.

It changes where it hides.

From network—
to identity.

From data center—
to cloud.

From infrastructure—
to policy.

But it remains.

Zscaler does not eliminate the core.

It exposes it.

It forces organizations to confront:

Where control actually exists.
Where dependencies still matter.
Where assumptions must be removed.

This is not a technological shift.

It is an operational one.

Because what is not understood—
will not be governed.

And what is not governed—
will not sustain control.

Reference

1. Rose, S., Borchert, O., Mitchell, S., & Connelly, S. (2020). Zero Trust Architecture (NIST Special Publication 800-207). National Institute of Standards and Technology. https://doi.org/10.6028/NIST.SP.800-207

Conclusion

Execution Defines the Outcome

This is the execution lens.

Not merely written—

but lived,

and left here

as record.

By the time a program reaches execution—

the decisions have already been made.

Architecture has been chosen.
Identity has been defined.
Applications have been mapped.
Control models have been designed.

What remains—

is not planning.

It is proof.

Proof that the system can hold
under real conditions.

Proof that access behaves
as it was intended.

Proof that dependencies
have not been misunderstood.

Because execution does not introduce reality.

It reveals it.

Zscaler does not create complexity.

It exposes it.

What was undocumented—
surfaces.

What was assumed—
breaks.

What was loosely controlled—
fails.

And in that moment—
the question is no longer:

"Was the architecture correct?"

The question becomes:

Was the organization prepared
to operate it?

Zero Trust is not validated
by design.

It is validated
by behavior.

Not in controlled environments.

Not in pilot groups.

But in production—
where inconsistency exists
and variation is unavoidable.

That is where execution separates:

Programs that move—
from programs that hold.

Because movement alone
is not success.

Control is.

This is where most transformations fail—
not at the point of decision, but at the point
where decision becomes discipline.

Execution requires:

Clarity of ownership.
Consistency of enforcement.
Alignment across identity, network, and endpoint—
and the ability to respond—
when the system does not behave as expected.

These are not new requirements.

They are the disciplines
this book has named,

chapter by chapter—
now standing together,
at the point where they are tested.

Without that—
architecture remains theoretical.

With it—
control becomes real.

Strategy defines direction.

Architecture defines intent.

Design defines possibility.

Execution defines the outcome.

Zero Trust is not declared.

It is enforced.

Zscaler is not deployed.

It is governed.

Transformation is not announced.

It is sustained—
under pressure.

Architecture can be perfect.

Strategy can be sound.

Intention can be aligned.

And still—
the program will fail
if execution does not hold.

That is the lens.

Not what was planned.

Not what was promised.

Not what was designed.

What held—
when everything was placed under pressure.

That is execution.

That is the outcome.

> ***That is the discipline—this book was written to make visible.***

Bonus Chapter

The Iron Point™

The Psychology of the Executor

Execution does not break under criticism.
It does not collapse under praise.
It holds.

Self-Acceptance Equilibrium Model™
Equipollent Leadership™ Research Series • 2026

There is a moment inside every high-stakes program—
when the architecture holds,
when the policies are enforced,
when the wave is in motion—

and someone says something that should not matter.

A skeptical executive.
A disappointed stakeholder.
A colleague who questions the approach.

And in that moment—
the decision is not technical.

It is psychological.

Does the executor hold—
or does the environment decide their worth?

This is the question that most leadership books fail to ask.
And the one that most execution programs fail to answer.

Not because the answer is unavailable.
But because it requires looking somewhere
most practitioners are not trained to look:
inward.

This chapter does not concern itself with Zscaler policy architecture.
It does not address wave sequencing, RAID governance, or cutover command.

Those disciplines have been covered.
They are necessary.

They are not sufficient.

Because no technical framework survives contact with a destabilized executor.

And no executor remains stable
without a foundation that holds
independent of external outcome.

That foundation has a name.

It is called The Iron Point™.

1. The Question Modern Psychology Left Unanswered

Modern psychology has spent decades attempting to elevate self-esteem.

Organizations invest in building it.

Schools seek to develop it.

Leadership programs devote entire curricula to strengthening it.

Yet a critical question is rarely asked:

> ***What happens when identity becomes dependent upon self-esteem itself?***
> — The foundational question of the Self-Acceptance Equilibrium Model™

The answer reveals a paradox that existing frameworks have failed to resolve.

Whether an individual possesses low self-esteem or high self-esteem—
both states remain vulnerable to the same fundamental flaw:

dependency on external evaluation.

One collapses under criticism.
The other expands under praise.

In both cases, the individual's sense of worth remains tethered—
to what others think,
to what outcomes produce,
and to what circumstances allow.

The dependency changes.
The vulnerability remains.

For the executor—
this is not merely a psychological observation.

It is an operational risk.

Because the enterprise environment is built to produce both.

Praise when the deployment succeeds.
Criticism when the rollback is called.
Pressure when the wave stalls.
Approval when the board is satisfied.

If the executor's stability is tethered to any of those outcomes—
the program is no longer governed by structure.

It is governed by whoever holds the most recent opinion.

This insight led to the development of the Self-Acceptance Equilibrium Model™—
and its central construct:

The Iron Point™.

2. The Research Foundation

The Iron Point™ Framework is not built on intuition alone. It is grounded in decades of peer-reviewed psychological research spanning clinical practice, leadership science, and human development.

2.1 — Self-Esteem vs. Self-Acceptance: A Critical Distinction

Academic research has consistently identified self-esteem and self-acceptance as related but meaningfully distinct constructs with different psychological effects.

> ***Self-esteem was more closely associated with affect, while self-acceptance appeared more closely associated with general psychological well-being and more helpful when undertaking clinical work for general psychological problems.***
>
> — MacInnes, D.L. (2006). Journal of Psychiatric and Mental Health Nursing. [1]

> ***Programs focused on self-acceptance improved well-being more than those targeting self-esteem. Self-acceptance buffers against the negative effects of social comparison.***
>
> — Orth, U. & Robins, R.W. (2022). American Psychologist, 77(1). [2]

2.2 — The Problem of Contingent Self-Esteem

Research by Crocker, Kernis, and Deci & Ryan established the concept of contingent self-esteem—a state in which self-worth fluctuates based on external outcomes. This is the precise mechanism that makes execution vulnerable.

> *Fragile self-esteem is unstable or contingent, and therefore easily threatened by criticism, rejection, or other negative events. People whose sense of self-worth depends on external validation, achievements, or accomplishments are more susceptible to the pursuit of self-esteem.*
>
> — Crocker, J., Lee, S.J., & Park, L.E. (2004). University of Buffalo Research Series. [3]

> *Contingent self-esteem is a form of ego involvement in which people focus on how successes and failures reflect on the self. Individuals who are ego-involved do things because they feel they have to, rather than because they want to.*
>
> — Deci, E. & Ryan, R. Scientific American. [4]

2.3 — The Case for Unconditional Self-Acceptance

The theoretical foundation of The Iron Point™ aligns directly with Albert Ellis's Rational Emotive Behavior Therapy (REBT), which introduced Unconditional Self-Acceptance as a cornerstone of psychological health.

> *Unconditional self-acceptance is the practice of accepting oneself fully despite flaws or failures. Ellis argued that many psychological disturbances stem from irrational beliefs tied to self-worth, where individuals believe they must perform well or be loved by others to be worthy. One's value as a person is not contingent on external conditions.*
>
> — Albert Ellis Institute / REBT Framework. [5]

Research further confirms that low levels of unconditional self-acceptance are strongly correlated with anxiety, depression, and low life satisfaction.

Conversely—
cultivating unconditional self-acceptance produces resilience,
emotional regulation,
and sustainable psychological stability. [6]

For the executor,
this is not a wellness concept.

It is a performance architecture.

3. The Equipollent Paradox

At first glance, low self-esteem and high self-esteem appear to be opposites.

One appears weak. The other appears strong.
One appears undesirable. The other appears desirable.

Yet when examined through the lens of psychological dependency—
both become functionally equivalent.

They are psychologically equipollent.

LOW SELF-ESTEEM	HIGH SELF-ESTEEM (Contingent)
Derives power from negative feedback	Derives power from positive feedback
Collapses under criticism	Becomes defensive under criticism
Craves approval	Depends on continued success
Identity defined by failures	Identity defined by achievements
Vulnerable to rejection	Vulnerable to failure

> Both states surrender psychological stability to forces outside the individual.
> Neither represents true freedom.

In an enterprise program environment—
both extremes produce the same outcome:

A decision-maker who cannot be trusted under pressure.

The low-esteem executor avoids confrontation.
Withholds the difficult truth.
Accommodates the stakeholder who should be challenged.

The high-esteem executor refuses to rollback.

Protects the timeline above the environment.

Escalates defensively when the architecture is questioned.

In both cases—

control is compromised.

Not by the platform.

Not by the architecture.

By the psychological state of the person responsible for executing it.

The Self-Acceptance Equilibrium Model™ maps this paradox—and the path beyond it.

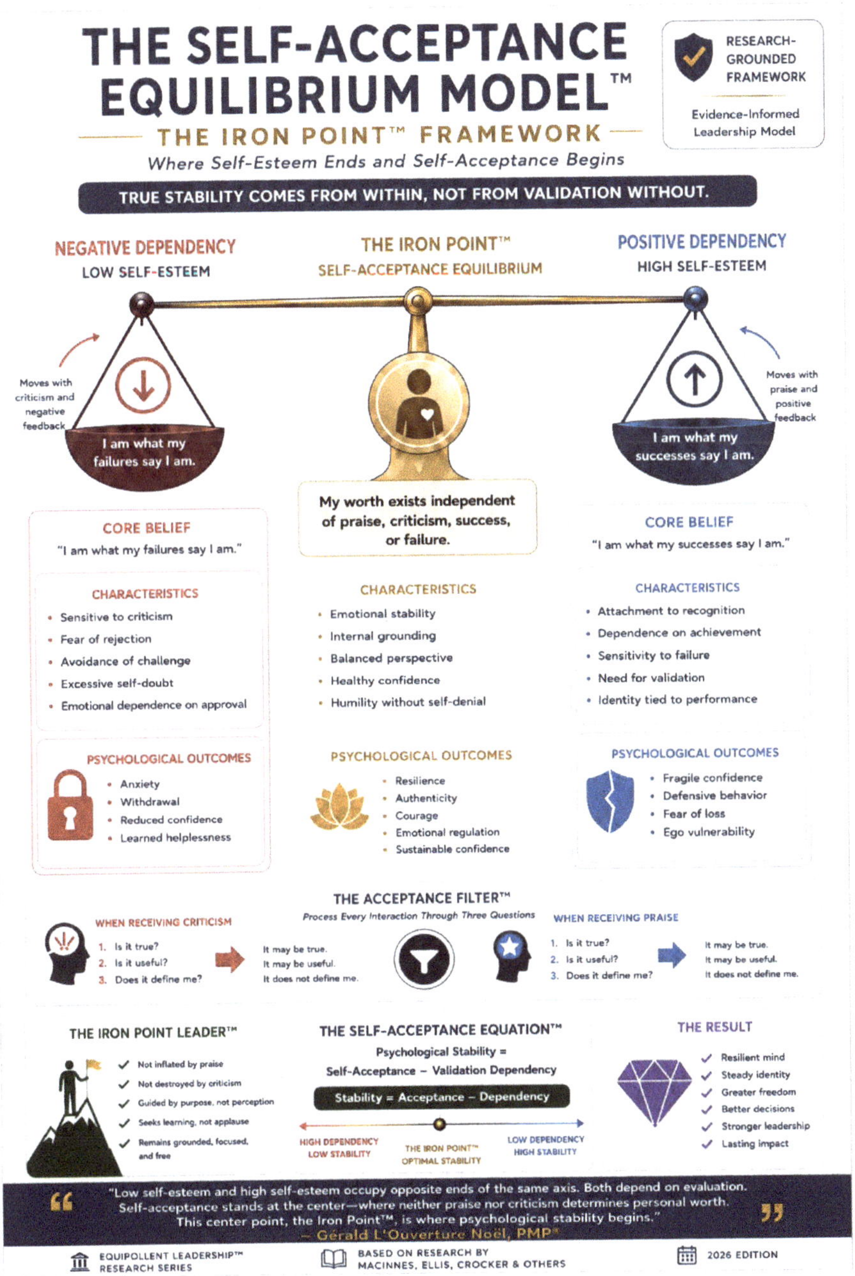

Figure B.1 — The Self-Acceptance Equilibrium Model™ • The Iron Point™ Framework • © Gérald L'Ouverture Noël, PMP® • Equipollent Leadership™ Research Series 2026

This is not a spectrum between two poles. It is an elevation above both—to a state neither extreme can reach.

4. The Three States of Human Identity

The Self-Acceptance Equilibrium Model™ identifies three distinct psychological states that govern how individuals experience and respond to their environment.

Each state produces a different category of executor.

And each produces a measurably different execution outcome.

STATE I

Negative Dependency

Low Self-Esteem

Core Belief

"I am what my failures say I am."

Characteristics

— High sensitivity to criticism
— Persistent fear of rejection
— Avoidance of challenge and risk
— Excessive self-doubt and self-blame
— Emotional dependence on others' approval
— External and interpersonal contingencies of self-worth

Psychological Outcomes

— Chronic anxiety and withdrawal
— Reduced confidence and initiative
— Learned helplessness
— Vulnerability to depression

STATE II

Positive Dependency

High Self-Esteem (Contingent)

Core Belief

"I am what my successes say I am."

Characteristics

— Strong attachment to recognition and titles
— Performance-dependent identity

— Hypersensitivity to failure
— Defensive behavior when challenged
— Chronic need for external validation
— Ego-protection responses to perceived threats

Psychological Outcomes

— Fragile and unstable confidence
— Defensive and aggressive reactions to criticism
— Fear of loss and status erosion
— Narcissistic tendencies under pressure

STATE III

Self-Acceptance Equilibrium

The Iron Point™

Core Belief

"My worth exists independent of praise, criticism, success, or failure."

Characteristics

— Stable sense of self, unaffected by outcomes
— Internal grounding and emotional balance
— Healthy, non-defensive confidence
— Genuine humility without self-denial
— Open to feedback without being controlled by it
— Identity anchored in values, not performance

Psychological Outcomes

— Psychological resilience
— Authentic and courageous action
— Consistent emotional regulation
— Sustainable, non-defensive confidence
— Growth orientation under pressure

5. The Iron Point™ Principle

The strongest psychological position
is not found at either extreme of the self-esteem spectrum.

It is found above that spectrum entirely.

> ***While self-esteem depends on evaluating how well we think we're doing—or how well people tell us we're doing—unconditional self-acceptance asks us to recognize that we're human. We perform well sometimes and poorly at other times, but these moments do not ultimately define us, or our worth.***
>
> — Psychology Today (2025). Have We Been Misled About Self-Esteem? [7]

The Iron Point™ represents a stable psychological state
where personal worth remains constant
regardless of external evaluation.

Research confirms that this state—
unconditional self-acceptance—
is not complacency or stagnation.

It is the foundation
from which genuine growth
and courageous action
become possible.

BEFORE THE IRON POINT™	AT THE IRON POINT™
"What do others think of me?"	"What can I learn from this?"
Identity is externally defined.	Identity is internally anchored.
Every interaction becomes a referendum on worth.	Every interaction becomes an opportunity for growth.
Decisions are made for approval.	Decisions are made for purpose.
Feedback is a threat.	Feedback is information.
Pressure produces collapse or defensiveness.	Pressure produces steadiness.

Applied to enterprise execution—

this means something specific.

The executor at The Iron Point™

does not require the board's approval to call rollback.

Does not require the vendor's validation to challenge the architecture.

Does not require the stakeholder's praise to enforce the policy.

Their stability is not situational.

It is structural.

6. The Acceptance Filter™

The Acceptance Filter™ is a practical three-question cognitive tool for processing both praise and criticism without allowing either to define personal worth.

Rooted in Ellis's REBT model and evidence-based cognitive restructuring, it creates a pause between stimulus and response.

In high-stakes execution environments, that pause is the difference between a reactive decision and a governed one.

PRAISE	1. Is it true? 2. Is it useful? 3. Does it define me? *It may be true. It may be useful. It does not define me.*
CRITICISM	1. Is it true? 2. Is it useful? 3. Does it define me? *It may be true. It may be useful. It does not define me.*

In practice, this filter does not require a quiet office or a reflective moment.

It requires a decision—

made in advance—

that outcome does not govern identity.

The executive who praises the deployment is not wrong to do so.

The stakeholder who criticizes the wave sequence is not necessarily right.

Both pieces of information can be received.

Evaluated.

Acted upon where useful.

And released where they are not.

This filter prevents two equally destructive responses:
the collapse under criticism that marks State I,
and the ego inflation under praise that produces the fragile executor of State II.

In both cases—
the individual remains the stable observer.
Not the passive recipient of an externally-assigned identity.

7. The Self-Acceptance Equation™

The mathematical relationship at the heart of this model can be expressed simply.

Psychological Stability = Self-Acceptance ÷ Validation Dependency

or, expressed more simply:

Stability = Acceptance − Dependency

As dependency on praise and criticism decreases—
psychological stability increases.

Research on contingent self-esteem confirms this inverse relationship:
the more self-worth is staked on external outcomes,
the more unstable and vulnerable the individual becomes. [3][4]

Conversely—
as unconditional self-acceptance increases,
dependency naturally diminishes.

The individual no longer requires external events
to confirm their worth.

They can receive feedback—positive or negative—
as information,
not identity.

And that distinction—
between information and identity—
is the operational difference
between a program that holds under pressure

and one that fractures beneath it.

8. The Iron Point Leader™

Leaders who operate from self-acceptance demonstrate a measurably distinct advantage.

This is not a theoretical assertion.

Research on leadership psychology and ego-involvement consistently shows that leaders whose self-worth is externally contingent make poorer decisions under pressure, exhibit more defensive and reactive behaviors, and are more susceptible to manipulation through flattery or criticism. [3][4]

VALIDATION-DEPENDENT LEADER	THE IRON POINT LEADER™
Makes decisions to gain approval	Makes decisions grounded in purpose and truth
Avoids feedback that threatens ego	Welcomes feedback as a source of growth
Becomes arrogant under praise	Remains grounded under praise
Becomes defensive under criticism	Remains steady under criticism
Surrounds themselves with those who validate	Surrounds themselves with those who challenge them
Leadership depends on continued external affirmation	Leadership is powered by internal conviction, not approval

Applied to the Zscaler execution environment—
this distinction is not abstract.

The validation-dependent program leader
defers rollback because a vice president is watching.

The validation-dependent project manager
withholds the RAID risk because it might seem like incompetence.

The validation-dependent technical lead
defends an architecture that has already revealed its flaws—

because acknowledging the flaw feels like acknowledging failure.

And in each case—
the program pays the price.

Not because of a platform limitation.
Not because of a design error.

Because one person's psychological state
became more important than operational control.

The Iron Point Leader™ does not operate this way.

Not because they are immune to pressure.
Not because they are indifferent to opinion.

But because their stability
is not located in what others think.

It is located in what they know.

And what they know—
is the mission.

9. The Iron Point™ in the Execution Environment

The Iron Point™ is not a credential.

It is not a certification or a title.

It is a psychological operating state—and it produces a specific category of execution behavior.

9.1 — When the Executive Pushes Back

The wave is in motion.

The data shows instability.

The risk threshold has been reached.

And the executive says:

"We cannot pause. We cannot afford the perception of delay."

Two types of executors exist in this moment.

The first accommodates—

because the executive's approval feels necessary for survival.

The second holds—

because the mission does not change based on who is watching.

The Iron Point™ executor is the second.

Not because they are reckless.

Not because they disregard authority.

Because they understand something the executive may not yet see:

Forcing a wave forward without control
does not protect the program.

It defers the damage.
And deferred damage always costs more than acknowledged risk.

9.2 — When the Rollback Is Called

Rollback is where psychological state becomes most visible.

The validation-dependent executor
delays rollback because rollback feels like failure.

The Iron Point™ executor calls rollback
because rollback is control.

As Chapter 14 of this manuscript establishes:
rollback is not retreat.
It is a disciplined return to a known stable state.

But that discipline requires something that governance frameworks alone cannot provide:

A leader whose identity
is not attached to the outcome.

Who can say—in front of the board, the vendor, the team—

"We are going back.
Because going forward would cost more than this moment.
And I am not interested in protecting appearances.
I am interested in protecting the environment."

That statement requires no approval to make.
It requires only that the leader's worth
is not located in whether the statement is applauded.

9.3 — When the Program is Criticized

Every program of consequence
attracts criticism.

Some of it is useful.
Some of it is political.
Some of it is timed to destabilize.

The Acceptance Filter™ was built for exactly this moment.

Is it true?
Is it useful?
Does it define the program's worth?

If the criticism is accurate—receive it.
Adjust the approach.
Do not collapse.

If the criticism is political—evaluate it.
Understand the source.
Do not become defensive.

If the criticism is designed to undermine—
recognize it for what it is.
Do not absorb it as identity.

In every case—
the executor remains the stable observer.

Not the passive recipient
of an externally-assigned narrative about the program's value.

10. Executive Insight

The objective of human development is not to create individuals with higher self-esteem.

The objective is to create individuals whose worth remains intact regardless of whether esteem rises or falls.

Low self-esteem and high self-esteem occupy opposite ends of the same axis.

Self-acceptance stands above that axis.

It is the point of equilibrium.

The point of resilience.

The point of freedom.

It is The Iron Point™.

A Zscaler program is not merely a technical undertaking.

It is an organizational transformation—
executed by people,
governed by people,
and ultimately sustained by the psychological stability
of the people responsible for it.

Architecture can be designed.
Waves can be sequenced.
Policies can be enforced.

But none of it holds
if the executor who governs it
requires the environment's approval

to function.

The Iron Point™ is not a guarantee of flawless execution.

It is the condition
under which flawless execution
becomes structurally possible.

Because when the environment pressures,
when the stakeholders question,
when the architecture reveals what was hidden—

the executor at The Iron Point™
does not ask what others will think.

They ask what the mission requires.

And then they act.

Without apology.
Without defensiveness.
Without the need for the environment to confirm
that they were right to do so.

That is the Iron Point Leader™.

That is the executor this discipline produces.

And that is where execution—
truly begins.

Bonus Chapter — Control Checkpoint

The conditions under which an executor can claim psychological readiness for high-stakes program governance.

An executor is operating at The Iron Point™ when:

— Rollback is called when the data demands it—not when the approval arrives.

— Criticism is received, evaluated, and acted upon without collapse or defensiveness.

— Praise is acknowledged, processed, and released without ego inflation.

— Difficult truths are surfaced to leadership regardless of anticipated reaction.

— Decisions are made on the basis of mission, not on the basis of perception.

— The program's worth is not redefined by a single failed wave or a difficult stakeholder.

— The executor's confidence is not contingent on the last meeting going well.

Psychological readiness is not announced.
It is demonstrated—
under pressure,
under scrutiny,
and under conditions designed to reveal
whether stability is structural or situational.

The Iron Point™ makes it structural.

* * *

Research References

The following peer-reviewed and authoritative sources ground the Iron Point™ Framework in established psychological science.

1. MacInnes, D.L. (2006). Self-esteem and self-acceptance: An examination into their relationship and their effect on psychological health. Journal of Psychiatric and Mental Health Nursing, 13(5), 483–489.
2. Orth, U., & Robins, R.W. (2022). Is high self-esteem beneficial? Revisiting a classic question. American Psychologist, 77(1), 5–17. https://doi.org/10.1037/amp0000922
3. Crocker, J., Lee, S.J., & Park, L.E. (2004). The Pursuit of Self-Esteem: Implications for Good and Evil. In A.G. Miller (Ed.), The Social Psychology of Good and Evil. University of Buffalo.
4. Deci, E.L., & Ryan, R.M. Research cited in: Self-Esteem Can Be an Ego Trap. Scientific American. https://www.scientificamerican.com/article/self-esteem-can-be-ego-trap/
5. Albert Ellis Institute. Unconditional Self and Other Acceptance. REBT/CBT Framework. https://albertellis.org
6. Popov, S. (2019). When is Unconditional Self-Acceptance a Better Predictor of Mental Health than Self-Esteem? ResearchGate. Based on: Chamberlain & Haaga (2001) Unconditional Self-Acceptance Questionnaire.
7. Psychology Today (2025, October). Have We Been Misled About Self-Esteem? Meaningfull Blog. https://www.psychologytoday.com/us/blog/meaningfull/202510/have-we-been-misled-about-self-esteem
8. Li, Y., Guo, L., Yang, G., & Wu, Y. (2025). Effects of self-acceptance on prosocial behavior: the mediating role of self-esteem. Frontiers in Psychology. DOI: 10.3389/fpsyg.2025.1643464
9. Ellis, A. (2005). The Myth of Self-Esteem. Prometheus Books. (Referenced in: Decoding Unconditional Self-Acceptance: A Qualitative Report, 2023.)

A Vulnerable Moment
of the Author

The Iron Point™ did not begin in a research paper.
It began in a childhood.

I. THE ORIGIN

From the age of seven, Gérald L'Ouverture Noël lived inside a family where love and compassion were often absent, and where, at times, open hostility—not indifference, but words and actions that diminished a child's sense of worth—came from many of the people who were meant to represent safety, including his own father. His father's refrain was simple and devastating:

"You will never be anything."

He was given no name that honored him. He was called "It." Like the child in Dave Pelzer's account of survival, he was made to feel that his existence itself was an imposition.

Yet his story was not entirely without light.

One person believed in him.

His mother.

A homemaker with not a modicum of formal education, she possessed little social influence and even less authority within the home. Her voice rarely carried the power to change the environment around her. Yet to Gérald, she became what Socrates was to philosophy—not because she possessed formal education, but because she possessed uncommon wisdom. She became his Socrates.

Her words were not powerful enough to silence the voices around him.

But they were powerful enough to keep another voice alive—the one within him.

In an abyss where nearly every voice sought to diminish his worth, hers arrived like a small parcel of light—quiet, fragile, yet unmistakably real. It did not remove the darkness. It reminded him that darkness.

Most children in that environment fracture. The self-worth that requires love to exist — collapses when love is withheld.

He did not fracture.

Not because he was immune to pain. But because something in him — unnamed at the time, unresearched, untheorized — held. The more the words came, the more he refused to be defined by them. The more the rejection mounted, the more he stood on an internal foundation that the external world could not reach.

> *The more you called me by derogatory words,*
>
> *the more I accepted myself.*
>
> *— Gérald L'Ouverture Noël*

What Ellis would later call Unconditional Self-Acceptance. What Crocker and Orth would document in peer-reviewed research. What this manuscript calls The Iron Point™ —

he had already found it.

Alone. At seven.

◆ ◇ ◆

II. THE PARADIGM

This is why the model is not merely a leadership construct. It is a survival architecture — one with the power to reach the child who is being called names in a hallway, the teenager whose family has made them feel invisible, the young person standing at the edge of a decision they cannot come back from.

The suicidal crisis is, at its core, an identity crisis. A belief—installed by others—that worth is conditional. That if the conditions are wrong enough, long enough, the self has no ground left to stand on.

> *The Iron Point™ says otherwise.*
>
> *Your worth was never theirs to give.*
>
> *Which means it was never theirs to take.*

While Ellis, Crocker, Popov, and a library of peer-reviewed researchers documented the science of self-acceptance—the author did not discover this paradigm in a journal. He inhabited it as a condition of survival. He did not choose this framework after studying the literature. He built it, intuitively and alone, because the alternative was to disappear.

That is the difference between a theory and a testimony.

◆ ◇ ◆

III. THE APPLICATION

The Iron Point™ Framework is presented in this manuscript as an execution discipline for enterprise program governance. And it is that. But its roots carry a wider claim.

The same internal architecture that allows a Technical Project Manager to call rollback under executive pressure—is the same architecture that allows a child to survive a home that has decided they are nothing.

The same Acceptance Filter™ that separates mission from perception in a war room — is the same cognitive discipline that separates a derogatory name from a self-concept in a childhood bedroom.

The model applies wherever identity is under attack.

> *It can help young people navigate identity crisis.*
>
> *It can lower the suicidal rate.*
>
> *It can reach the child who has not yet been told*
>
> *that their worth was never contingent on anyone's approval.*
>
> — *The Author*

Gérald survived what many do not—not because his circumstances were merciful, but because he discovered, before anyone taught him, that his identity did not live in their hands.

He has now written it down.

So that others—especially the young, especially the ones being called "It"— might find that ground before the cost of searching for it becomes too high.

If there is a child somewhere reading this
who has been told they are nothing—

this story, told plainly,
may be the sentence that saves them.

Gérald L'Ouverture Noël

Appendix A

Glossary of Acronyms & IT Jargon

The terms below appear throughout this manuscript. Definitions are written in the context in which the term is used in the book — that is, as they apply to a Zscaler Zero Trust program — rather than as dictionary definitions. Entries introduced in the Bonus Chapter are marked accordingly. Entries are listed in alphabetical order.

INSTALL vs. IMPLEMENT — A Semantic Distinction

Throughout this manuscript, these terms carry specific operational meaning:

Install — To embed as a permanent, self-sustaining organizational capability. Installation means the organization owns, operates, and evolves the discipline independently, without dependence on the project team or external support. What is installed remains and endures.

Implement — To execute a project or plan; to carry out a defined initiative with a beginning, middle, and end. Implementation is the process of getting something done within a defined timeframe.

Zero Trust fails when organizations treat it as an **implementation** (project) rather than an **installation** (discipline). Until Zero Trust moves from "implemented project" to "installed operational discipline," it remains fragile and vulnerable to decay under pressure.

This distinction determines survivability.

A

ADKAR	Awareness, Desire, Knowledge, Ability, Reinforcement. A change-management model developed by Prosci that describes the five sequential outcomes individuals must achieve for an organizational change to succeed. In this manuscript it is applied as an execution discipline to drive Zero Trust user adoption.

Android	Google's mobile operating system. Referenced in the endpoint strategy chapter alongside iOS, iPadOS, and ChromeOS as a mobile platform whose enforcement behavior differs from desktop endpoints and must be governed through MDM rather than GPO.

API	Application Programming Interface. A defined set of rules and endpoints that allows one software system to communicate with another. Zscaler exposes APIs for configuration, log streaming, and integration with SIEM, ITSM, and identity platforms.

AWS	Amazon Web Services. A public cloud platform commonly used to host enterprise workloads that must be reachable through ZPA application segments.

Azure	Microsoft's public cloud platform. Frequently referenced alongside AWS and GCP as a destination for private workloads accessed through Zscaler Private Access.

B

BA	Bachelor of Arts. An undergraduate academic degree (used here in the author's credentials line).

BYOD	Bring Your Own Device. A policy under which employees use personal laptops, tablets, or phones to access enterprise resources. BYOD endpoints typically lack full management and require special posture and access treatment in a Zscaler deployment.

C

C2	Command and Control. The communication channel an attacker uses to direct compromised machines (often malware beaconing to an external server). ZIA threat protection inspects outbound traffic for C2 patterns.

CA	Certificate Authority. The trusted entity that issues, signs, and revokes digital certificates within a Public Key Infrastructure. Zscaler uses an intermediate CA for SSL inspection.
CAB	Change Advisory Board. The governance body that reviews and authorizes changes to production systems under ITIL-aligned change management.
CASB	Cloud Access Security Broker. A control point that enforces security policy between users and cloud services (typically SaaS). CASB capabilities are part of the broader SASE/SSE category alongside ZIA.
CBT	Cognitive Behavioral Therapy. A structured, evidence-based psychotherapeutic approach that examines the relationship between thoughts, feelings, and behaviors. Introduced in the Bonus Chapter in the context of the Acceptance Filter™, which is rooted in REBT — a framework Ellis developed as a precursor to and foundation of modern CBT.
CDN	Content Delivery Network. A geographically distributed network of servers that caches and serves web content close to end users. CDN endpoints often appear as third-party dependencies during application discovery.
CIO	Chief Information Officer. The executive accountable for an organization's information technology strategy and operations.
CISA	Cybersecurity and Infrastructure Security Agency. The U.S. federal agency under the Department of Homeland Security responsible for national cybersecurity guidance, including Zero Trust maturity models.
CMDB	Configuration Management Database. A repository that stores authoritative records of IT assets, services, and their relationships. Many enterprises lack a complete CMDB, which is why operational discovery is required for ZPA segmentation.

CPU	Central Processing Unit. The primary processor in a computer. ZCC and other endpoint agents are evaluated for CPU and memory overhead during readiness.

ChromeOS	Google's lightweight desktop operating system for Chromebooks. Treated in the manuscript as a mobile-class endpoint — managed through MDM, with constrained enforcement paths relative to traditional Windows, macOS, or Linux desktops.

D

DICOM	Digital Imaging and Communications in Medicine. The standard protocol for transmitting, storing, and retrieving medical imaging data. Referenced in the manuscript as an example of a clinical system that expects routable network-layer reachability and therefore resists clean ZPA application-layer brokering.

DLP	Data Loss Prevention. The set of policies, controls, and inspection techniques that prevent sensitive data from leaving the organization through web, email, or cloud channels. DLP is enforced through ZIA.

DNS	Domain Name System. The internet directory service that resolves human-readable names (such as example.com) into IP addresses. DNS behavior is critical to Zscaler traffic forwarding and to ZPA application resolution.

E

EDR	Endpoint Detection and Response. A class of security agent that continuously monitors endpoint activity for threats and supports investigation and response. Referenced in the manuscript as one of the resident endpoint agents (alongside ZCC and legacy VPN clients) that must coexist on the device during transition.

Equipollent Leadership™	A proprietary research framework introduced in the Bonus Chapter by Gérald L'Ouverture Noël, PMP®. The term 'equipollent' refers to psychological equivalence — the finding that low self-esteem and high contingent self-esteem, though appearing as opposites, produce the same operationally dangerous outcome: a decision-maker whose stability is dependent on external evaluation. The Equipollent Leadership™ Research Series grounds The Iron Point™ Framework in peer-reviewed psychological science.

F

FQDN	Fully Qualified Domain Name. A complete domain name that identifies a specific host, service, or application within DNS. In ZPA environments, FQDNs are commonly used to define application segments and brokered application access policies.

FQDN-based Segmentation	An application segmentation approach in which access policies are defined through Fully Qualified Domain Names rather than network-level IP reachability. This model aligns with ZPA's application-layer enforcement architecture.

FWaaS	Firewall as a Service. A cloud-delivered firewall capability that replaces traditional on-premises firewall appliances. Referenced in the manuscript as one of the converged services within the SASE/SSE category alongside SWG, CASB, and ZTNA.

G

GCP	Google Cloud Platform. Google's public cloud, often referenced alongside AWS and Azure as a destination for private workloads accessed through ZPA.

GPO	Group Policy Object. A Microsoft Windows mechanism for centrally distributing configuration, software, and security settings to domain-joined endpoints. GPO is one of several deployment paths for the Zscaler Client Connector.

GRE	Generic Routing Encapsulation. A tunneling protocol used to forward traffic from a corporate network egress point to the Zscaler cloud. One of several traffic-forwarding methods alongside IPSec, PAC, and ZCC.

H

Hybrid	In this manuscript, hybrid refers to architectural coexistence — not delivery methodology. It does not describe a blend of Agile and Waterfall. It describes the simultaneous operation of modern access models (such as Zscaler ZIA, ZPA, and ZCC) alongside legacy network-layer access (such as VPN) and traditional infrastructure dependencies. Chapter 15 establishes hybrid as a stable, governed state — not a transitional condition or a failure to modernize. The distinction is made explicit at the start of the chapter to prevent the common methodology reading of the term.

HTTP	Hypertext Transfer Protocol. The foundational application-layer protocol of the web. Referenced in the manuscript as the unencrypted predecessor to HTTPS; HTTP traffic is subject to category and policy enforcement at ZIA without requiring SSL inspection.

HTTPS	Hypertext Transfer Protocol Secure. HTTP traffic encrypted using TLS/SSL. HTTPS sessions are subject to SSL inspection in ZIA when policy requires content-level visibility.

I

ICMP	Internet Control Message Protocol. The network-layer protocol used by diagnostics such as ping and traceroute. ICMP behavior often differs between legacy VPN paths and ZPA, which can affect troubleshooting.

IdP	Identity Provider. The system of record for user identity and authentication (for example, Okta, Microsoft Entra ID, or Ping). Zscaler integrates with the IdP through SAML or OIDC, with user and group synchronization through SCIM.

IP	Internet Protocol. The addressing and routing protocol that underlies the internet. An IP address uniquely identifies a host on a network and is one possible (though less preferred) way to define ZPA application segments.
iOS	Apple's mobile operating system for iPhone. Referenced in the endpoint strategy chapter as a mobile platform where ZCC enforcement, certificate distribution, and tunnel persistence behave differently than on desktop OSes.
iPadOS	Apple's tablet operating system, derived from iOS. Treated in the manuscript as a mobile-class endpoint with the same enforcement constraints as iOS — MDM-managed, with operating-system-controlled networking behavior.
IPSec	Internet Protocol Security. A suite of protocols that authenticates and encrypts IP traffic, commonly used to build site-to-site tunnels. IPSec is one of the supported traffic-forwarding methods to the Zscaler cloud.
ISBN	International Standard Book Number. The globally recognized identifier assigned to a published book for cataloging and distribution. Referenced in the copyright page of this manuscript.
ITIL	Information Technology Infrastructure Library. A widely adopted framework of best practices for IT service management, including change, incident, and problem management. The Change Advisory Board operates under ITIL-aligned governance.
ITSM	IT Service Management. The discipline (and the class of tools, such as ServiceNow) used to manage the end-to-end delivery of IT services. ITSM platforms integrate with Zscaler for ticketing, change, and monitoring workflows.

L

LAN	Local Area Network. A network confined to a single building, campus, or trust boundary. Referenced in the manuscript as the historical context for which many legacy protocols (SMB, RDP, LDAP, NetBIOS) were designed — and which legacy VPN improperly re-creates for remote endpoints.

LDAP	Lightweight Directory Access Protocol. The protocol used to query and modify directory services (most commonly Active Directory). Cited as a legacy protocol designed for trusted LAN environments whose direct network exposure VPN re-enables and ZPA refuses.

Linux	An open-source operating system family. Referenced in the endpoint strategy chapter as one of the desktop endpoint platforms (with Windows and macOS) where full administrative control and consistent enforcement of forwarding profiles are typically available.

M

M&A	Mergers and Acquisitions. Corporate events that introduce previously separate identity, network, and application environments into the program — a common source of edge-case populations during Zero Trust rollout.

macOS	Apple's desktop operating system. Referenced alongside Windows and Linux as a desktop endpoint platform that supports MDM/GPO-style enterprise management, predictable certificate trust distribution, and stable ZCC tunnel persistence.

MDM	Mobile Device Management. A platform used to enforce configuration, security, and application policy on managed mobile and desktop endpoints. MDM is a primary deployment mechanism for the Zscaler Client Connector.

MFA	Multi-Factor Authentication. An authentication method that requires two or more independent verification factors (for example, password plus one-time code or hardware token). MFA cadence directly affects Zero Trust user experience.

MTU	Maximum Transmission Unit. The largest packet size, in bytes, that a network path will carry without fragmentation. MTU mismatches between legacy paths and Zscaler tunnels can cause subtle performance failures.

N

NetBIOS	Network Basic Input/Output System. A legacy session-layer protocol used by older Windows networking services for name resolution and resource sharing. Cited in the manuscript as a legacy protocol designed for trusted networks that VPN re-enables at the network layer.

NIST	National Institute of Standards and Technology. A U.S. federal agency that publishes widely adopted cybersecurity standards, including SP 800-207 on Zero Trust Architecture.

NISTIR	NIST Internal Report (or Interagency Report). A publication series from NIST. NISTIR 8286A, cited in the manuscript, addresses cybersecurity risk and enterprise risk management.

NSS	Nanolog Streaming Service. The Zscaler component that streams transaction logs from the Zscaler cloud to an on-premises or cloud SIEM in near real time.

O

OAuth	Open Authorization. An open standard for delegated authorization between applications without sharing credentials. OAuth 2.0 is the framework on which OpenID Connect is built and is referenced in the context of Zscaler's IdP integration.

OIDC	OpenID Connect. An identity layer built on top of OAuth 2.0 used for federated authentication. OIDC is one of the protocols by which Zscaler integrates with an IdP.
OpenID	An open identity standard. Referenced in the manuscript as the family of standards underlying OpenID Connect (OIDC), used for federated authentication between an IdP and Zscaler.
OpenVPN	An open-source VPN protocol and the associated client implementations (including commercial distributions such as Viscosity). Cited in the manuscript as the underlying technology of the incumbent VPN solution that Zero Trust is replacing in a real-world execution scenario.
OS	Operating System. The base software (Windows, macOS, Linux, iOS, Android, etc.) running on an endpoint. OS mix and version are key inputs to endpoint readiness and certificate trust planning.
OSI	Open Systems Interconnection. The seven-layer reference model used to describe network communications. In this manuscript, the VPN–ZPA comparison describes different access models—not an assertion that either technology uses only one OSI layer. Traditional IPsec and full-tunnel remote-access VPNs generally extend Layer 3 network reachability. Access may then be constrained through routing, transport-layer ports, firewalls, segmentation, and application controls. ZPA provides application-centric, identity-aware, policy-brokered access. Private applications may use web or non-web protocols, including TCP- and UDP-based services, while access is defined through application destinations, ports, protocols, identity, device posture, and contextual policy. The distinction is therefore between granting network reachability and granting access to an authorized application—not between technologies that operate exclusively at isolated OSI layers.

	Some legacy systems remain difficult to transition when they require dynamic network behavior, discovery, broad protocol access, server-initiated communications, broadcast or multicast functions, or dependencies that cannot be represented as stable application destinations.

OT	Operational Technology. Hardware and software that monitors or controls physical processes — common in manufacturing, utilities, and logistics environments. OT environments are typically high-friction populations during Zero Trust rollout.

P

PAC File	Proxy Auto-Configuration file. A small JavaScript file that tells a browser or operating system which proxy (such as the Zscaler cloud) to use for a given URL. PAC is one of the supported traffic-forwarding methods alongside GRE, IPSec, and ZCC. (The term is industry shorthand rather than a strict acronym.)

PKI	Public Key Infrastructure. The combination of certificate authorities, certificates, key material, and trust stores that supports authentication and encryption. PKI underpins Zscaler's SSL inspection and client-to-cloud trust.

PMBOK	Project Management Body of Knowledge. The Project Management Institute's reference standard describing project management processes, knowledge areas, and good practice.

PMI	Project Management Institute. The professional association that publishes PMBOK and administers the PMP certification.

PMO	Project (or Program) Management Office. The organizational function that governs project delivery, standards, and reporting across the enterprise.

PMP	Project Management Professional. A globally recognized project management certification administered by PMI.

PRE-MORTEM	A structured planning exercise in which the team imagines that the program has already failed and works backward to identify what caused the failure. Used in the manuscript as the upstream discipline that surfaces risk before RAID has anything to govern.

R

RAID	Risks, Assumptions, Issues, Dependencies. A program-control framework for tracking the four categories of signals that determine whether execution holds under pressure. The manuscript treats RAID as an active, real-time control model rather than a static log.

RDP	Remote Desktop Protocol. Microsoft's protocol for remote graphical access to a Windows host. Cited as one of the port-level services VPN exposes at the network layer before the application itself can authenticate the requester.

REBT	Rational Emotive Behavior Therapy. A psychotherapeutic framework developed by Albert Ellis that identifies irrational beliefs — particularly those tying personal worth to external performance or approval — as the root cause of psychological disturbance. Introduced in the Bonus Chapter as the theoretical foundation of the Acceptance Filter™ and The Iron Point™ Framework. Ellis's core construct of Unconditional Self-Acceptance — the recognition that personal worth is not contingent on outcomes, praise, or criticism — is the psychological architecture underlying the Iron Point Leader™ model.

S

SaaS	Software as a Service. Cloud-delivered applications consumed over the internet (such as Microsoft 365, Salesforce, or ServiceNow). SaaS traffic is governed by ZIA — URL filtering, threat protection, DLP, and SSL inspection are enforced before the user reaches the SaaS tenant.

SAML	Security Assertion Markup Language. An XML-based standard for exchanging authentication and authorization data between an IdP and a service provider. Zscaler uses SAML to federate authentication with the enterprise IdP.
SASE	Secure Access Service Edge. An architectural model that converges networking and security functions (SWG, CASB, ZTNA, FWaaS) into a cloud-delivered service. Zscaler is a leading SASE/SSE platform.
SCIM	System for Cross-domain Identity Management. An open standard for automating the provisioning and de-provisioning of user identities and groups between an IdP and downstream systems such as Zscaler.
Shadow IT	Cloud services and SaaS applications adopted by business units without IT involvement, oversight, or registration in the CMDB. Cited in the manuscript as a primary source of undocumented dependencies that Zscaler exposes during application discovery.
SIEM	Security Information and Event Management. A platform (such as Splunk) that aggregates and correlates logs and security events from across the enterprise. SIEM is a primary destination for Zscaler NSS log streams.
SMB	Server Message Block. The file- and print-sharing protocol used by Windows networking. Referenced in the manuscript as a legacy protocol that VPN places inside the trust boundary it was designed for, in contrast to ZPA's application-level brokering.
SOP	Standard Operating Procedure. A documented, repeatable procedure that defines how a routine task or response is to be performed.
Source IP Anchoring	A Zscaler ZIA mechanism that preserves the originating source IP address of traffic leaving the Zscaler cloud, allowing IP-allowlisted third-party services to continue functioning during a VPN-to-ZPA transition. Cited in the manuscript as a real-world coexistence control for legacy IP-bound integrations.

SP	Special Publication. NIST's designation for technical publications. SP 800-207 is the foundational NIST document on Zero Trust Architecture.

SSE	Security Service Edge. A cloud-delivered security architecture model focused on secure access, web protection, CASB functionality, Zero Trust access enforcement, and data protection services delivered from the cloud edge.

SSH	Secure Shell. A protocol for encrypted remote command-line access to a host. Cited as one of the port-level services that legacy VPN exposes at the network layer before identity-aware enforcement is applied.

SSL	Secure Sockets Layer. The historical predecessor to TLS, still commonly used as shorthand for both. 'SSL inspection' in Zscaler refers to the controlled decryption, inspection, and re-encryption of TLS-encrypted traffic at ZIA.

SWG	Secure Web Gateway. A control point that inspects and filters outbound web traffic for policy, threat, and data-loss enforcement. SWG functionality is one of the converged services within SASE/SSE, delivered through ZIA in Zscaler's platform.

T

TAC	Technical Assistance Center. The vendor support function (here, Zscaler TAC) that owns escalation and platform health diagnosis.

The Acceptance Filter™	A proprietary three-question cognitive tool introduced in the Bonus Chapter for processing praise and criticism without allowing either to define personal worth. Rooted in Ellis's REBT model and evidence-based cognitive restructuring, the filter consists of three questions applied to both praise and criticism: Is it true? Is it useful? Does it define me? In high-stakes execution environments, this filter creates a pause between stimulus and response — the difference between a reactive decision and a governed one.

The Equipollent Paradox	A concept introduced in the Bonus Chapter describing the psychological equivalence of low self-esteem and high contingent self-esteem. Though appearing as opposites, both states make the executor vulnerable to the same operational risk: decision-making governed by external evaluation rather than mission. The Equipollent Leadership™ Research Series formally documents this paradox as the foundational problem The Iron Point™ resolves.
The Iron Point™	The central proprietary construct of the Bonus Chapter. The Iron Point™ represents the psychological state of Unconditional Self-Acceptance — a condition in which personal worth remains stable and intact regardless of external praise, criticism, success, or failure. Named for its structural stability under pressure, it is the operating state from which the Iron Point Leader™ governs. In the execution context, The Iron Point™ is the condition under which rollback can be called without defensiveness, difficult truths can be surfaced without fear of approval loss, and mission can be served independent of stakeholder perception. It is not a credential or title — it is a demonstrated psychological state.
The Iron Point Leader™	A proprietary leadership archetype introduced in the Bonus Chapter. The Iron Point Leader™ is an executor whose psychological stability is internal rather than externally contingent — one who makes decisions grounded in mission and truth rather than in the need for approval, recognition, or validation. Contrasted with the Validation-Dependent Leader, the Iron Point Leader™ remains steady under both praise and criticism, calls rollback when the data demands it rather than when the approval arrives, and surfaces difficult truths to leadership regardless of anticipated reaction.
The Self-Acceptance Equilibrium Model™	A proprietary psychological framework introduced in the Bonus Chapter, developed by Gérald L'Ouverture Noël, PMP®. The model maps three psychological states — Negative Dependency (low self-esteem), Positive Dependency (high contingent self-esteem), and Self-Acceptance Equilibrium (The Iron Point™) — and establishes that the first two, despite appearing opposite, are functionally equipollent in execution environments. The model is grounded in peer-reviewed research from Orth & Robins (2022), Crocker, Lee & Park (2004), Deci & Ryan, and the Albert Ellis Institute's REBT framework.

TLS	Transport Layer Security. The cryptographic protocol that secures traffic on the modern internet (the successor to SSL). The manuscript uses 'SSL inspection' as the customary industry shorthand for the controlled decryption, inspection, and re-encryption of TLS-encrypted traffic at ZIA.

TPM	Technical Project Manager. The execution role at the center of the manuscript — accountable for translating architecture intent into controlled, sequenced delivery across infrastructure, identity, and endpoint teams.

U

URL	Uniform Resource Locator. The full address used to retrieve a resource on the web. URL filtering is a category-based access control enforced by ZIA.

V

Viscosity	A commercial OpenVPN client developed by SparkLabs for macOS and Windows. Cited in the manuscript as the specific incumbent VPN client in a real-world execution scenario that was migrated to a Zero Trust posture through ZPA.

VPN	Virtual Private Network. A legacy remote-access model in which an authenticated user is placed onto the corporate network through an encrypted tunnel. The manuscript repeatedly contrasts VPN's network-level reachability with ZPA's application-level access.

W

Wildcard Domain	A domain specification using a wildcard character (for example, *.example.com) to match multiple subdomains under a parent. In ZPA, wildcard domains expand the scope of an application segment beyond a single FQDN — useful for breadth, but with reduced precision relative to explicit FQDN definitions.

Windows	Microsoft's desktop and server operating system family. Referenced in the endpoint strategy chapter as the dominant managed-desktop platform — supporting GPO, MDM, certificate trust distribution, and consistent ZCC enforcement.

X

XML	Extensible Markup Language. The structured, tag-based document format used by SAML assertions exchanged between an IdP and Zscaler during federated authentication.

Z

ZCC	Zscaler Client Connector. The endpoint agent installed on user devices that enforces policy and forwards traffic to ZIA and ZPA. ZCC is the component that makes Zero Trust enforcement consistent across networks.
ZDX	Zscaler Digital Experience. The Zscaler module that provides end-to-end visibility into user experience, application performance, and network path quality. Used heavily during validation and stabilization.
ZIA	Zscaler Internet Access. The cloud-native secure web gateway that governs all outbound internet and SaaS traffic, providing URL filtering, threat protection, DLP, and SSL inspection.
ZPA	Zscaler Private Access. The Zero Trust Network Access service that brokers application-level access to private applications, replacing network-level reachability provided by traditional VPN.
ZTNA	Zero Trust Network Access. The architectural pattern of granting access to specific applications based on identity and context rather than placing the user on a network. ZPA is Zscaler's implementation of ZTNA.

Index

Zscaler: Through the Execution Lens™

"Execution is not the last step. It is the only step that counts."

This index covers the principal terms, frameworks, disciplines, and execution models referenced throughout the work. Page numbers refer to the final manuscript pagination. Where a concept appears across multiple pages in continuous treatment, a range is given (e.g., 108–125). Where the same term surfaces in distinct discussions across separate parts of the manuscript, page numbers are listed individually, separated by commas.

Entries are organized alphabetically by letter section. Cross-references formatted as "See" direct the reader to the principal entry under which a concept is fully developed. "See also" references point to related entries that extend or complicate the primary treatment. Proprietary frameworks introduced in this work — including the Execution Lens™ itself—are indexed both by their full name and by the operational context in which they are formally established.

The Execution Lens™ is not a product. It is a discipline—a way of reading every architecture decision, every stakeholder dynamic, every rollback trigger, and every wave boundary through the question of whether execution, not design, is being served. Entries in this index reflect that orientation. Terms that might appear technical in isolation — RAID, ADKAR, ZPA, PKI — are indexed here as execution instruments, not as abstractions. The reader who uses this index well will find not just where a term appears, but how it functions inside a program under real conditions.

A

B

C

D

E

F

G

H

I

L

M

N

O

P

R

S

T

V

W

Z

www.ingramcontent.com/pod-product-compliance
Lightning Source LLC
LaVergne TN
LVHW071335210926
848486LV00003B/155